BECOMING
SPECTACULAR

BECOMING SPECTACULAR

THE RHYTHM OF RESILIENCE
FROM THE FIRST
AFRICAN AMERICAN ROCKETTE

JENNIFER JONES
WITH LATOYA SMITH

AMISTAD

An Imprint of HarperCollins*Publishers*

The names and identifying details of some of the individuals mentioned in
this book have been changed to protect their privacy.

HarperCollins books may be purchased for educational, business, or sales
promotional use. For information, please email the Special Markets
Department at SPsales@harpercollins.com.

FIRST EDITION

Designed by Janet Evans-Scanlon
Unless otherwise noted, photographs are provided by the author.
Illustration on page iii © Roisa/stock.adobe.com.
Photograph on page 70 courtesy of the Daily News.

Library of Congress Cataloging-in-Publication Data has been applied for.

978-0-06-327037-4

24 25 26 27 28 LBC 5 4 3 2 1

I dedicate this story with love and gratitude to the incredible mentors, dance teachers, family, and friends who guided and supported me on my journey to success. Their unwavering belief in me helped shape the performer I had always aspired to be.

I pay tribute to the fearless pioneers who broke barriers, championed diversity, and continue to dream boldly in the face of adversity. Your sacrifices and perseverance are honored in these pages and inspire future generations to fearlessly pursue their dreams.

For the Rockettes—past, present, and future. Honoring the African American Rockettes who danced beside me, who succeeded me, and who are yet to grace the stage. Embracing a community of diversity and mutual respect. Grateful for our shared journey of dreams and inclusion. Thank you for being part of my spectacular journey.

Warm appreciation extends to the unsung heroes backstage—the dedicated stagehands, meticulous dressers, visionary costume designers, talented orchestra members, and hardworking crew. Their tireless efforts bring each performance to life with care, precision, and heartfelt commitment. They form the foundation of every spectacular moment onstage.

To all the dreamers and believers who dare to push boundaries and chase their dreams with unwavering faith, this memoir stands as a beacon of hope and validation. Remember, "becoming spectacular" is not just a dream but a reality for those who believe in themselves.

CONTENTS

My first *Christmas Spectacular*

1

Shattering Glass Ceilings, One Kick at a Time

Making history rarely feels like it in the moment. We anticipate something remarkable and humbling, a time for people to pause, take notice, and celebrate. A monumental event of sorts. But people often only see how far a person has come, and not the obstacles put in their path along the way. There are countless groundbreaking people of color who are often acknowledged, but many who are not. Many whose stories are left untold.

When hardships happen to them, we want to believe that any "first" must know the journey they're embarking on. That they understand the discipline, faith, and determination it takes to push through. The unfortunate truth, however, is that this is not always the case.

In fact, this is rarely how it happens.

I know from experience that most "firsts" are people who simply want to do what they love: find that cure, write, sing, act, or dance.

As a dancer, I believe there is no greater feeling than the one I have when I'm at the barre, stretching and going over routines in my head. A stillness washes over me, and everything but the music fades to black. When I'm not in a studio or on a stage, I crave the dopamine that flows through my veins upon accomplishing a more challenging move. There's no feeling like it.

Since I was nine, my world has revolved around motion and the exhilaration that comes from unlocking new levels of achievement and performance.

On January 31, 1988, I made my national debut with the world-famous Radio City Rockettes at the NFL Super Bowl halftime show in San Diego. It's no exaggeration or cliché to say that it was an impossible illusion made real for my younger self, who desperately wanted to succeed as a dancer and performer. It's like those stories we grew up on, where a fabled person is thirsty in the middle of the desert, and the mirage they thought was a figment of their imagination—something they could only see—is finally here.

I became the first Black Rockette in sixty-three years.

And I wasn't the only person making history that day. Chubby Checker was performing with us in the Radio City–produced halftime show. In 1960 he had revolutionized pop music with a new dance crazy that swept the nation: the twist. Doug Williams was about to become the first Black quarterback to play in a Super Bowl ever. He led the Washington Redskins (currently named the Washington Commanders) to win the Super Bowl, passing for four touchdowns in a single quarter. To say it was a night of history is an understatement, and I was a part of this iconic moment.

But I'm getting ahead of myself.

While there was plenty of excitement around the day, I had no idea that my performing at the Super Bowl would matter to anyone or that this was such a charged year in NFL history. In my eyes, I was only a dancer looking to do what I loved in one of the biggest ways possible. Unbeknownst to me, the 1988 Super Bowl came at the end of a season that had been shortened by a players' strike. In September of the previous year, starting players on almost every football team in the country had walked out of their locker rooms with demands that included free agency and pension benefits. This had been a belabored topic of conversation—the strike didn't come out of thin air. In fact, many of the franchise owners had known the strike was coming and had begun to prepare backup rosters to undercut players' demands. As the then owner of the Dallas Cowboys, Tex Schramm, allegedly told the executive director of the players' union, "You guys are cattle and we're the ranchers, and ranchers can always get more cattle."

///////

For all the talk of the First Amendment, I know it can be difficult to find your voice when you're confronting power. After just one cancelled week of pro football, replacement players were out on the field. The 1987 NFL season experienced a more than 20 percent drop in both television viewership and in-person attendance, so the impact of the strike was certainly felt. However, since fill-in players were willing to take the field and some veterans agreed to cross the picket line, owners took their chances in order to save money and the season.

I knew none of this because I was—and still am—a girl's girl. I have no concept of football dynamics and certainly not the politics and decisions made behind closed doors. What I know now—and what I've seen at other times in my career—is that when there is nothing to gain, progress comes slow.

In the 1980s, affirmative action initiatives aimed to promote diversity in the workforce, but faced challenges and pushbacks. Some organizations resisted these efforts, leading to debates and tension. The era highlighted the complexities and controversies surrounding these programs, emphasizing the importance of ongoing support for inclusivity and equality in workplaces and communities.

By the time of my Super Bowl appearance, internal entertainment industry politics were still hidden to me. I was as green as blades of fresh-cut grass in the summer. I didn't know how power was held or meted out. What I did know was that the world was changing, and I was a part of that major shift. Black people were taking center stage at one of the most "American" days of the year. People of all races around the country would soon be crowding around televisions and radios, and for once Black people would be crucial to this celebrated day. I couldn't get caught up in the symbolism of what my inclusion meant, because I had a job to do. Which meant I was a lot more focused on my big break and needing to prove myself to my new employers than what was happening around me.

///////

San Diego's energy was intoxicating. My welcome letter read "The city of San Diego is alive with Super Bowl Fever, and everyone has been anxiously awaiting the arrival of the Rockettes." And I believed them. The city was abuzz with anticipation for the game, and we felt like rock stars.

My then roommate and fellow dancer Maria Hill and I became fast friends as we went over our moves. In a sea of more seasoned girls, it was comforting to be with another newbie. Radio City kept our days busy, which helped me stay focused. The Rockettes are a precision dance troupe with a deeply rooted reputation, so we had to be perfect. A not-so-unofficial motto we have is that you're only doing your job if you're attracting no attention.

Perfection and uniformity are musts, because if any dancer does more or less than the woman standing next to her, it disrupts the illusion that people love so much. Many don't know that the Rockettes troupe was based on a British dance company of the late nineteenth century called the Tiller Girls. Dancers were recruited according to a strict height-and-weight requirement and proficiency in tap, ballet, and jazz dance. Their performances featured straight lines and what Russell Markert, the founder of the Rockettes, called "intuitive mathematics." After seeing the Tiller Girls perform in 1922, Markert claimed, "If I ever got a chance to get a group of American girls who would be taller and have longer legs and could do really complicated tap routines and eye-high kicks, they'd knock your socks off." The vision was set for a chorus line of women who move and appear as one.

As a Black woman, I stand out anywhere I go. Brown skin. Long legs. Wide eyes. Curly hair. As a matter of fact, I was born standing out, arriving in a world where the media and popular culture favored whiteness. In an industry that prioritized white fans and families, uniformity sold. I needed to work overtime to ensure that my first time onstage with the Rockettes wouldn't be my last.

When we weren't rehearsing for hours on end, production had us on nonstop press and publicity trips. My parents and Patricia, my younger sister whom we called Peaches, had flown out to San Diego to be with me, but it was only in spirit, because I never had time to see them. During press tours I didn't speak much about myself, though the reporters did try to dig and get into the racial part of things. Instead, I kept the interviews focused on my excitement to be a part of such an outstanding organization, despite rumored racial tensions behind the scenes. Markert had once been quoted as saying, "If a girl got suntanned and she was alongside a girl who could not get the sun, it would make her look like a colored girl." And then later, Rockettes choreographer Violet Holmes infamously and publicly stated, "One or two Black girls would definitely distract. You would lose the look of precision, which is the hallmark of the Rockettes." Reflecting on it now, I am deeply concerned by the notion that the Rockettes were not evaluated based on talent but rather on racial identity, which points to a troubling systemic and institutionalized racism within the performing arts. The historical context of the Rockettes' founding as the Missouri Rockets in 1925 highlights a time when Black performers were unjustly prohibited from dancing alongside white performers, underscoring the pervasive inequality that permeated the entertainment industry. It's important to recognize and honor the pioneering contributions of Black dance companies and individuals such as Arthur Mitchell, Katherine Dunham, and Geoffrey Holder, who challenged these discriminatory norms and opened doors for greater diversity and inclusivity in the world of dance and performance. Their legacies serve as a reminder of the ongoing need to confront and dismantle structural barriers in order to create a more equitable and inclusive creative environment.

Radio City's top brass worked hard to ensure I answered the questions I was asked to their liking. They were strategic in getting the media to move beyond Violet's words, focusing on me becoming a trailblazer and not on how it might affect the Rockettes' uniformity. None of that bothered me, because I knew nothing of the Rockette history, and I was there to dance. I didn't need a red carpet rolled out for me or think pieces picking apart how and why I came to be the first to validate my existence. It was my first big job, and that's what I was focused on. So as our group was bused around from press junkets to the San Diego Zoo to local water parks, I never lost sight of what I was truly there for. I knew dance was my life, and if what they needed from me was a smile and laughter at a few official Rockette activities, I would do that. Any spare second I had, I was rehearsing or going over dance formations in my head.

A few days later, I arrived at Jack Murphy Stadium (fondly referred to as "The Murph") and was directed to a special backstage entrance for those performing in or directing the night's activities. Though the stadium was demolished in 2020 to make way for the Snapdragon Stadium now owned by San Diego State University, I'll never forget its magnitude or how cold it was. The hairs on the back of my neck stood at attention and made sure I didn't get too comfortable.

As I passed the trailers, looking for my dressing area, I took in the scale of this production. There were hundreds of trailers, it seemed, and thousands of performers and production staff buzzing around making sure Radio City Music Hall would be able to maintain its reputation for precision by the end of the evening. And when I say thousands, I'm not exaggerating. Radio City doesn't like to be outdone, so our twelve-minute performance included the tireless preparation and work of four hundred band members. The concept for the year 1988 was taken quite literally. There were forty-four Rockettes, which equaled eighty-eight legs; eighty-eight pianos with eighty-eight pianists and even eighty-eight keys on the piano; two college marching bands; and the hit singer Chubby Checker with his own team. Between the people, instruments, equipment, costumes, and props, we were jam-packed.

To save time (and space), most of the Rockettes came dressed, "done up," and needed only to stretch. Our costumes were designed to dazzle, and that they did. Adorned with a gold-and-white-sequined leotard perfectly bedazzled, with a bow tie to match, I was ready for my close-up. We would perform two numbers, and I soon learned the art of mastering getting dressed in sixty seconds or less. Because it was so chilly, I had on burgundy sweatpants and a white sweatshirt with palm trees on the front to keep warm until it was showtime.

Any dancer knows that overthinking is your worst nightmare. You have to get into and stay in the right state of mind to be able to perform with excellence. You know how they tell you not to pull an all-nighter right before an exam because you won't actually learn much more but instead tire yourself out? It's true. But when you hear the crowd roaring and whistles being blown and everyone around you is practicing, you become more anxious than you already were and feel compelled to do something with that energy.

Our producers called a thirty-minute call to performance, then a fifteen, and I began to loosen up, knowing that our time was nearing. Rookie mistake, because with a performance at an athletics game, time is sure to get pushed back. Sure enough, between timeouts and flags, the halftime performance was way behind schedule. The anticipation was rising, and it took everything in me not to jump on one of those trailers and scream out, "Let's do this already!"

Instead of making myself crazy, I allowed my mind to wander and grounded myself in the moment. That may sound ironic or even contradictory, but being too focused on the technicality of the moves would make me lose the elements that made for an enjoyable performance. I had to loosen the reins on my thoughts in order to execute the way I needed to move, similar to meditation.

I thought of Peaches and Cheryl, my other sister, who sandwiched me both in age and love. They have always seen me as a whole, multifaceted human being with ambition and trepidation, longing and desire. I reminisced about the deep belly laughs and late-night tears we'd shared. There aren't many people who can relate to the childhood we experienced and the worldview we have. Brown dots in a white world, wading into the water, refusing to be invisible. It was their fortitude and resilience that I held close to me in the moment I needed them most.

I also thought of my parents, who weren't able to be at the stadium and knew prior to boarding their plane that they wouldn't be able to come inside yet still traveled across the country to watch their middle baby girl. At that time, promoters weren't handing out VIP or backstage passes to anyone outside of the performers, so my family had to watch the show from their hotel room. I thought of my father, skin as deep brown as the Mississippi earth he comes from, dependable and immovable. My dad, who has always been stuck in his ways. And my mother, with her skin as pale and white as hibiscus—sweet like hibiscus, too. Of them coming together and choosing me; earth and flower giving each other meaning and making each other possible. Offering their comfort and support leading up to one of the most important days of my life. I relished the buttress they provided, because I knew that it hadn't always been this way.

I thought of my mom, sitting on her bed late one afternoon while I was getting settled at home after dance class, and her poking and prodding worriedly. All I wanted to do was make her proud, and all she could do was look at me with a frown of worry. I was desperately trying to show her my new moves from Frank Hatchett's dance class and the new eight count that I couldn't get enough of. My mother was concerned and kept asking me about my future plans, even though I kept answering, "Dance." Those lines in her forehead would deepen, her lips would purse up, and she would shake her head and ask the question in a different way. I didn't show her my routine that day, but I understood her concern.

She was a mother wanting the best for her daughter, knowing that the world wasn't always kind to those who did what they loved. This world wanted efficacy and productivity, a purpose that benefited others. My mother's only thought was *How can dance pay her bills or offer stability?* The unspoken part was *How can a Black girl find stability in this line of work?* There weren't many examples of those without connections making it in this business, and my parents had seen enough of the world to know that.

I thought of my dad dropping me off at the train station and saying this would be the last time he would be giving me money. I heard the resistance in his voice. The loving parent beneath the stern one telling me what he thought I needed to hear to break me out of a childhood dream. I remembered closing his car door and feeling the opposite of how they had hoped. I wasn't ready to accept that maybe it was time to put my dance shoes back in my closet and do something more realistic. On the contrary, I recalled making mental notes to hustle harder for my own place and resources. It was clear I'd need to make this a reality with my own two feet, a challenge I was willing to take on. What I wasn't willing to do was deny what my heart was telling me and trade in passion for pushing a cog forward.

To me, any human existence is miraculous, and I didn't intend to waste my time on this planet. No, I'd simply have to work harder. Now here I was on the other side of that hard work, hoping and praying it was enough. The Rockettes meant so much more to me than just a career move. They represented independence and affirmed, at a time when I needed the assurance most, that my gut was worth trusting. I had something to say and a gift to offer. Joining a company as established as Radio City meant that I could show my parents I was doing well, validate my choice to pursue dance, and step into a life of fulfillment knowing that I didn't choose it at the expense of my livelihood. Our society incentivizes people to quell the fires within them in favor of walking a straight, safe path. That never interested me, and, thankfully, it was paying off. Tonight would be the proof.

At last, my train of thought was interrupted when the end of the first half was finally announced and places were called. We threw off our sweats and got into formation as production rushed to set the field with all eighty-eight grand pianos and other instruments, and I quickly reviewed the run of the show in my head.

The pianists opened the set, followed by the entrance of the San Diego State and University of Southern California marching bands to "The Super Bowl Super-Band Swing." The end of that song would be our cue to run out and perform to Duke Ellington's "It Don't Mean a Thing (If It Ain't Got That Swing)" and into George Gershwin's "I Got Rhythm." We opened the dance standing inside a large piano box and held poster boards shaped like piano keys that we were supposed to let fall on our particular counts. Once the music began, we stood still, waiting for our cue, arms going a bit numb from a combination of the cold weather and nervous energy while clenching our keys. The moment our music started, I dropped my board and pranced out onto the field, in awe of the more than seventy thousand people filling the stadium. It was magical.

I occasionally glanced back at the grand piano players behind me having what looked like the time of their lives, banging on those keys, and everything felt electrifying and almost spiritual. They, too, belonged on this field. You could see in their confident smiles that these people had nurtured the love they had for the piano until it swelled into this gift. When we started the infamous kick line that the Rockettes are known for, our legs moving seemingly in perfect unison and as high into the air as the birds, the stadium roared into thunderous clapping and whooping. In church, it's the act of so many minds and hearts homed in on a specific feeling that catches like wildfire. Being on that field made me feel like we could lift the entire stadium into the air and just vibe out for a lifetime. It was then that something clicked. I realized the importance of precision, uniformity, and teamwork. The performance felt effortless as the movements flowed out of my body divinely, and the crowd clapped and cheered along to our upbeat rendition of classic songs. I was enamored with the applause and didn't want the moment to end.

As we made our way off the field and out of sight, we high-fived and hugged one another like *we* had just won the game. Three hundred cheerleaders then stormed the turf, accompanying Mr. Checker and his most beloved song, "Let's Twist Again," to close the set out. Twelve minutes of high energy and a pounding chest.

After both numbers, I felt an immense sense of joy and fulfillment. I knew deep within that I had made the soulful choice of following my intuition. Being in that glorious spotlight ignited a fire in me, affirming that it was my calling and the path I was meant to tread. The sheer bliss and contentment I experienced in those fleeting moments validated my decision to pursue this artistic journey wholeheartedly, allowing my intuition to guide me and lead me toward my passion. I believe that we are put on this earth on purpose and for a purpose. That purpose becomes revealed to us over the course of our lifetime, and it's clear when we've chosen the right path, because everything falls into place.

There's an ease to finding what you were born to do. It doesn't mean there won't be hard work and diligent effort to be applied. But, rather, doing what you love will make you want to work harder.

What is surprising about this is how natural it feels and how aligned the world becomes to support you. There's something euphoric about dancing as if no one is watching, even while knowing that the world is doing exactly that.

///////

As we boarded our buses back to the hotel, everyone around me began to celebrate and talk about their future plans. I knew for several reasons that I was headed right back to my hotel. For one, my family had traveled all this way, and I wanted to finally spend time with them. But secondly, and more importantly, I wasn't out of the woods. Though this was an awesome opportunity, it didn't secure me a spot on the *Christmas Spectacular* roster that would perform for the holiday season in New York City each year. After a job well done, I was unsure if I would get another chance to perform with them, since I had only been hired for that one show. This made me uncertain about what my next job would be and what my future held. Isn't that something? Even when making history or just making progress, we are so fixated on what comes next, it distracts us from living in the moment.

I did not know a whole lot about the Rockettes or their history. However, throughout my time there, I would learn dance history, the history of the Rockettes, and the institutional and systematic racism that preceded me. I was so naïve.

I'm not anymore, and now is the time for me to tell my story.

I hope to inspire individuals to pursue their dreams despite challenges or uncertainty about the future. Or for anyone who may not have a clear path but feels driven to follow their instincts and intuition.

I always knew I wanted to dance.

But I had no idea that my life would take me on such a journey. No idea that I would be considered a "first" story when all I was doing was fulfilling a childhood dream. It's now my responsibility to talk about that journey. To share my trials and tribulations, in the hopes that someone can learn from the lessons, setbacks, and hardships that I've had to overcome in my life.

What I wish I could tell the nineteen-year-old me is to be present. To fully immerse myself in my first big break. To allow the sounds and smells and feelings of that experience to envelop me. I have danced on hundreds of stages, thousands of times. You never get another "first."

On that fateful evening in January, I wanted to be present and enjoy the moment, but I knew I had a long several months ahead of me to snag one of the coveted spots on the Rockettes lineup. Preparation plus opportunity. I couldn't afford to get comfortable yet.

As I packed my clothes and readied myself to head back home to New Jersey, I thought back on the performance and the feeling I had when I was surrounded by the other dancers. "God wouldn't bring me this far to not bring me all the way." I said it partly as a prayer and mostly to convince myself. As Grandma Jones always said, "Prayer changes things."

In October of that year, I would get the official call from Violet Holmes to come in to perform for the Christmas show.

My prayers had been answered.

In spite of those months being painstaking, there was a harvest waiting for me in the end, a harvest born of the seeds I'd been planting for years. Looking back, I'm surprised I was shocked to get that call. I had worked my butt off to make it to that stage, and I deserved to be there as much as anyone else. It was time to give myself some credit. Many will glamorize the wins without honoring the uncelebrated work that is necessary to get there. I had to focus and do the work before I could set foot on any major stage. Every grueling workout proved to be incredibly worth it, because there is no replacement for consistency. More than that, no matter what anyone else says or what they consider "realistic," your vision was handmade just for you. Build your inner voice and self-trust so that you can tune out the rest of the noise. On the other side is the life you've been waiting for.

2

Enter: The Backstage Door

Before I tell you about that Rockette audition, I think it's important that I start with where I began. I am the daughter of an interracial couple, and I was born in 1967 in Belleville, New Jersey, at Clara Maass Medical Center. By the time I was born, my older sister, Cheryl, was a year old. I can't remember Cheryl and me ever being at odds. My earliest memory of her is that we were inseparable. Best friends, really. Way more than sisters. Since she was older, she was more of the caretaker. So I was pretty much following her lead, you know? We always played together, whether it was hopscotch, jump rope, or hand games, and looked out for each other during the hard times. Like when my parents fought, and we would comfort each other. Or when I didn't get that audition I wanted. Or when another boy broke my heart.

My mother, Linda Jane Lourie, was born and raised in Rockaway, New Jersey, to Anglo parents whose worst nightmare was for her to end up with a dark-skinned Black man from the South. My father, Booker Thaddeus Jones, was born in 1940 in Mississippi, though his family had deep roots in Alabama. During the Great Depression, despite its hardships, his parents, Laura Brooks and Booker T. Jones Sr., managed to secure a stable life. Their diligent work ethic saw them juggling several jobs simultaneously, including tending to a small farm where they cultivated vegetables and raised chickens. This self-sufficiency ensured that they remained unaffected by the financial struggles of the era and had sufficient resources to weather the storm. Laura initially worked as a nurse before becoming an educator, while Booker Sr. returned from World War II to take on the role of a security guard. When my father went on to attend college and realized his parents were having a hard time paying for his education, he opted to go into the military. My aunt had moved from the South some time ago to become a nurse and lived in Newton, a small town in New Jersey. After my dad completed his service, she told him to come to Jersey, because there were plenty of opportunities for work in the factories. She knew a pastor who could give him a place to stay and help get him a job. Upon careful consideration—moving to the North was a huge step, leaving everything and everyone he knew behind—my dad took his sister up on her offer.

During his off days, the pastor would take my dad around to look for jobs. A couple weeks later, my father landed a full-time position at a place called Greystone, which was a mental institution in Morris Plains. There he worked in the kitchen washing dishes and performing cleaning duties. The job wasn't difficult, and he was grateful for the opportunity. New Jersey was nothing like Mississippi, and my dad was a bit shy. Leaving his day job, he'd walk forty-five minutes to his part-time position, where he worked nights as a dishwasher at a diner called Sip & Sup. The two jobs offered him the ability to send money home to his family still living in Mississippi. A short time after his arrival, he met my mother at the Sip & Sup.

My mother was immediately attracted to my dad, although he was quiet and kept his head down, washing dishes and performing his duties at the restaurant. She told one of her fellow waitresses to tell my father she liked him. One day, at the end of her shift, she offered him a ride home since he didn't have a car. She learned he had sold it to send money to his parents. Drawn deeper into their connection by his selflessness, they became an item from that point on.

Despite interracial couples being more accepted in today's world, this was the 1960s, so it was still a bit of a taboo subject that ended up at the Supreme Court with the *Loving v. Virginia* decision. For the first year of their relationship, my mother kept it a secret from her parents, because she knew they wouldn't be happy. Since she was living in an apartment on Main Street in Rockaway with her best friend, this was easier to do. My mother said she had the time of her life living with her best friend, exploring, dating, working, and just being a carefree young adult without someone constantly looking over her shoulder.

When their lease was up a year later and her friend decided to move out to marry her boyfriend, my mother begrudgingly moved back home with her parents. Returning home made it difficult to hide her relationship, especially since my parents were getting pretty serious. This would only add to the complex dynamic between my mother and grandfather, whom we affectionately called

PaPa. They had had a strained relationship when my mother was growing up. No one could tell my mother, who had always been headstrong, what she could or couldn't do, much less whom she could date. Besides, falling in love and wanting to build a life with someone shouldn't be a bad thing. So she sat her parents down and told them.

PaPa wasn't thrilled. In fact, he told her she should go see a therapist. My mother hesitated at first but agreed. During her first session, she told the doctor that she was just a woman in love. When the therapist suggested a joint session with everyone, my mother agreed. She went home and told her parents that there was nothing wrong with her, that the therapist said everything was their fault, and that she wasn't going to change her mind about dating my father.

She never went back to therapy again.

When my dad asked for her hand in marriage a short while later, she accepted and moved out of her parents' home into an apartment in Newark with him.

The dynamic between my mother's and father's parents was an interesting one. They were on completely opposite ends of the spectrum. My father's family never treated my mother any differently, and they were very open to the relationship. They were just happy my father found love, and they adored my mother. Throughout numerous historical instances of redlining, segregation, and gerrymandering, there have been white individuals who do not accept or wish to live with or be around people of color, particularly African Americans. It's important to clarify that I am not referring to all white or Black people, but rather sharing my personal experience and what I have observed in my life, particularly as a biracial woman. Thankfully, my mother never allowed her parents to stand in the way of their union, and she became Mrs. Booker T. Jones Jr. in July 1965.

The rift between my mom and her parents lasted a good while before she and my father married. Afterward, my grandparents came around and accepted my father. They were thrilled when they learned my mother was pregnant with Cheryl a year later. I am glad they were able to reconcile their differences because my grandparents were an important part of my childhood and upbringing.

My earliest childhood memory was growing up on North Ninth Street, a predominantly Black neighborhood. Newark was just making a comeback after the 1967 riots, started in response to the brutal beating of a Black cabdriver by police officers that summer. It was once a prominently white neighborhood, but post–World War II, whites began moving to the suburbs, since many of them could afford a car and mortgage via the G.I. Bill. Through the Great Migration, more Blacks were moving from the South to the North and Midwest, just as my dad had. The term "white flight" became increasingly common as people observed advertisements promoting better homes and mortgages in the suburbs while also witnessing the migration of Black individuals to Newark. Unfortunately, as state and local governments focused on "white flight," the cities were being neglected, losing a tax base that could fund programs, including schooling, and other necessary tools to keep neighborhoods afloat. For these reasons, within decades, Newark quickly moved from one of the US's most prominent cities to one of its most poverty- and crime-stricken.

My mother was eight-and-a-half-months pregnant with me, and Cheryl was fourteen months old. My mom kept the shades pulled down and the house quiet for fear that someone would break into our home and harm us. My dad would go out to work but made sure he got home before curfew. Yes, you read that right. There was a citywide curfew in place to try to keep things from escalating, since most of the rioting was happening after-hours. He told me there were a couple nights when he was stopped by the police on his way home, and they would ask, "Where you headed, boy?" Thankfully, once he showed his ID and respectfully said he was only going to and from work, they let him through with no problems. But as you know, this was still a dangerous occurrence, and my mom was always afraid that one day, his luck would run out, and he would be one of many harassed, assaulted, or even killed by police. Once the conflict had abated, over two dozen people were dead, hundreds more injured, and property was damaged for decades. Despite its historical context, my dad quickly found his groove in Newark—workwise, at least—and started his own sewer cleaning business, which he and my mother would run together.

He had always been a hard worker and had gotten the idea after watching a program on our local PBS station. With his experience in the military and doing odds-and-ends jobs throughout his life, he was confident that he could be a successful entrepreneur. Sewer cleaning was a trade that he could learn and eventually master. He got a loan from the Small Business Administration and got a van and equipment. The SBA was giving out loans to minorities in Newark after the riots.

Mom would take the service calls, and my dad would go out to do the jobs. The business flourished rather quickly, and soon, my parents were able to afford to move us to a house in Hillside, which is where I started kindergarten. This was a prominent Black neighborhood, too, and all was going well for us . . . at least financially. My father was making great strides in the business and had always been good at saving money. Now he was getting more trucks on the road and hiring servicemen. This was a 24/7 operation. Before beepers, my dad would need to find a pay phone after work to call my mom about any new jobs before coming home. Sometimes, right after he got back and relaxed, he'd have to rush out again for another call. When beepers were around, my mom could page him, but she still had to wait for him to find a pay phone for updates while he was on a job. The financial gain allowed us to participate in extracurricular activities like dance classes, baton twirling classes, horseback riding lessons, and other enriching opportunities. However, with it also came challenges.

Navigating change within a marriage can be likened to climbing a mountain. As you ascend, the landscape around you shifts, presenting new challenges and opportunities for growth. Sometimes the path ahead may seem steep and arduous, testing your patience and perseverance. But with effective communication, mutual support, and a shared vision of reaching the summit together, each step forward can strengthen your bond and ultimately lead to a rewarding and fulfilling journey. If communication breaks down, support falters and visions diverge; moving through those changes can become treacherous and potentially lead to disaster. Understanding and working through these stages are crucial for a successful ascent, and I think my parents were on a descent.

I was maybe six or seven when they took my sister and me out to dinner at a Chinese restaurant. Cheryl and I were having a great time until my parents started arguing in harsh whispers. I honestly don't even remember what they were arguing about. I just know that Cheryl and I leaned into each other, coming up with a game plan. Cheryl said, "You say whatever Mom says, and I'm gonna say whatever Dad says." I don't know why, but we thought this would be the funniest thing ever. And so we did just that. We looked at each other like we were having a conversation, going back and forth, word for word, copying everything they said and how they said it. I remember my parents stopping, looking at us, and realizing how ridiculous they sounded. Because immediately after, they burst out laughing, and Cheryl and I joined them. For a good five minutes, we just laughed and laughed—I mean, soul-deep, tears-in-your-eyes laughter. And that ended their argument. We had a really good time that night in spite of how it started.

My grandparents NaNa and PaPa had a lovely home in Rockaway with a garden full of fruits. We loved picking and enjoying the sweet apples and tasty rhubarb. NaNa always had sugar ready for us to add to the rhubarb, since the taste was slightly bitter. The grapevine and currant bush promised even more colors and flavors. NaNa canned her fruits, so we enjoyed eating her homemade jams and jellies on toast for breakfast when we stayed the night. Visiting their home felt like a celebration of good things and left us feeling happy and warm.

My mom got us involved with the local community center, where we did baton twirling and gymnastics. I remember, for one parade, we had to do a baton twirling routine. We had to spin the baton up in the air, turn around, and catch it. The entire time, all I could think about was not dropping it, and yet I dropped it anyway.

This is also when I began tap-dancing at Joe Rudy's dance studio. He was a tall, thin, patient Italian man who would teach me what would become my favorite tap step—back flaps. This is when you swing your foot forward, coming from the front or diagonally, hitting the ball of your foot in a tap step.

Getting ready for classes or shows always took a little extra time, as my mother didn't quite know how to handle or have the patience to style our beautiful, curly black hair. She never let us go out looking any kind of way, but sometimes she spent so much time on our hair, she'd often wrap hers into a scarf. I know this seems like a cliché, but it's a very real issue in many interracial children's lives. Hair is a part of your identity, a part of what makes you feel beautiful, feel connected to your roots. When one is made to feel that their hair is inadequate or unattractive, it can negatively impact one's mental well-being. Grown women have been known to feel shame about their hair—hence the variety of documentaries, books, articles, and hair care lines that exist to help women of color care for their hair. My mother thought she was being funny when she'd say things like "I need a whip and a chair to tame your hair."

Though I hadn't really known what she meant, I began to feel self-conscious, not understanding why mine was so hard to tame. Her best friend's daughter's hair seemed perfect. It was always styled like Farrah Fawcett's hair, feathered to perfection. This was also the time when Whoopi Goldberg famously joked about putting a towel around her head and pretending it was long hair in one of her stand-up comedy segments. I wished my hair could look like Farrah's, but wishful thinking did not yield results.

"I am done with this," my mother said one morning before school. "You're getting a haircut."

Since my mom loved short Afros, she thought I would look great with that style. After searching for a good salon, she finally found one.

I honestly thought she was kidding, but my mom was dead serious about taking my sister and me to the salon when school let out that day. On the way there, I pleaded with her, but she wouldn't listen. I covered my face and cried the entire time I sat in the chair, begging my mother not to let that woman cut off my hair. I think the stylist felt badly, because she kept asking if I was okay, trying to cut and style my hair as quickly as possible. When she showed me my image in the mirror, I was horrified and angry with my mother. I could not believe she had forced me to cut off my hair. I *hated* that haircut. The short Afro made me look like a boy. I wanted to dissolve into myself and just disappear right off the face of the planet. When we got home that night, my dad assured me that it would grow back, just not in time for school the next day. I thought this was the worst day of my life.

The next day, I cried my way to school. I remember my mother and I standing in line, waiting to go inside the school building, and I was just crying and crying. Holding on to my mother's legs, I tried to prevent her from taking me inside. I just knew all the kids would make fun of me. I thought I looked so ugly. Even my teachers felt sorry for me and did their best to coax me into school. "Come on, baby girl, it looks good. You look so cute. Just come inside. Don't you worry." But I was devastated. So much so that my mother finally gave in and took me home. All I could think about was that I couldn't wear my favorite hairstyle—two ponytails, half up, half down. I used to love that style, but now all my hair was gone.

A few years went by, and my hair did grow back. I was about ten years old, Cheryl eleven. By this point my parents were arguing pretty frequently. As a child, you never really know what adults fight about; you just know they're your mom and dad, and you want them to be happy. My parents decided to move us to Randolph for a fresh start. It was also when they had my sister Patricia, whom we called Peaches. She was the planned child, conceived by our parents during a stable time in their marriage. They hoped she would bring them closer together and mend their relationship's differences.

As a family, we looked forward to going out for Sunday brunch once a month. It was a tradition my father would instill in us. We were excited when the Hilton hotel opened nearby. I remember our first visit there, when we got dressed up and got to decide if we wanted to order from the menu or have the buffet, which featured hundreds of items. I always chose the buffet because I could make my own omelet, eat delicious Belgian waffles, and enjoy lots of fruits and bacon. Walking around and looking at all the different foods made me feel grown-up, especially with the seafood and cheese options. At the end of our meal, we would relax at the table, enjoying coffee and orange juice while chatting and laughing. We'd leave the Hilton feeling satisfied. My sister and I would spend the rest of the day playing games while our parents took a nap, happy from our special brunch together.

Just before our move, while the house was being built, I was preparing for what would become one of my fondest memories in school: my fourth-grade recital. We were performing to songs from the 1940s, and my teacher Mr. Juliano had chosen *me* for a leading part even though I was one of the shyest kids in class. He told us that we were going to do the jitterbug to "Boogie Woogie Bugle Boy." There were six couples chosen to do the dance as our class-mates stood in line behind us and sang the words. I was required to come to school early or stay late for practice. I don't know why my teacher picked me, since I was so quiet, but I'm happy he did. After we learned the jitterbug dance, we practiced the alphabet song while standing in a semicircle. Mr. Juliano would hand letters up onstage to me, and I would pass them down to the group.

The day of the recital, I remember being so nervous, but I loved doing the jitterbug, and my partner and I didn't miss a step. After-ward I walked to my spot on the stage to start the alphabet song. When the show was over, everyone came up to me and was like, "You were so good. You did a great job." What I felt cannot be explained. As I danced and performed on the stage, it was as if I had found my true home. The music and lyrics enveloped me, and I moved with a freedom that made me forget an audience was watching me.

This was the beginning of my love for the performing arts.

After the recital, my parents—who were always big Broadway theatergoers—wanted to share their love of the stage with us. They would often go out on the town for dinner and to see the latest shows, like *Pippin* starring Ben Vereen, *Hair* with Melba Moore, *Jesus Christ Superstar*, and *Oh! Calcutta!* Given my newfound pas-sion, they invited us to join them on the Great White Way, which is what they called the lit-up streets of Broadway. When they got us tickets to see *The Wiz* at the famed Majestic Theatre, it was the perfect introduction to the grand stage. It was a kid-friendly show with an all-Black cast.

Cheryl and I were so excited to get dressed up and go to Manhattan. This was about a year or so before Peaches was born. Upon walking inside, we saw the bustle of ushers, bartenders, and show patrons buzzing around, dressed to the nines. People dressed up to see a show back then, much like everyone used to dress up to travel. The theater was adorned in rich burgundy and gold, making it feel like a grand ballroom. No matter where you sat, you were always in the perfect seat. The intricate details on the ceilings, doors, and other accents left me in awe. From giving our tickets at the counter to receiving the playbill and being escorted to our seats by the ushers, it was an experience that has stayed with me throughout my life.

As we sat and listened to the orchestra warm up with the curtains drawn, I could barely contain my excitement. While waiting for the show to begin, I found myself wondering what the actors had done that day; had they taken a dance class or gone to the supermarket, or were they warming up right at that moment? My mind was filled with question after question. Then, as the orchestra began the overture and the lights dimmed, my heart raced with anticipation. I could hardly wait for the show to start. For the next two hours, we were transported into the magical world of Oz.

When Mabel King sang "Don't Nobody Bring Me No Bad News," I couldn't take my eyes off her. She was larger than life and commanded the audience's attention with her strong vocals.

And Stephanie Mills . . . words can't even describe how she captured everyone with her alluring voice and superb acting skills—a force to be reckoned with. Her rendition of "Home" had the theater silent. The stage setup, scenery, makeup, dancing, the costumes . . . the Munchkins being wheeled around on stools to make them short. Many may not know, but Phylicia Ayers-Allen Rashad costarred as a Munchkin in the show.

After the show ended, everyone in the audience jumped out of their seats and applauded. I remember clapping so fast and hard, my hands tingled. Upon exiting the theater, we waited near the backstage entrance and were lucky to catch a glimpse of some of the cast members, like Hinton Battle, André De Shields, Tiger Haynes, and Mabel King, hanging out casually, as if it was just another day. Then Stephanie Mills appeared, and the crowd was filled with excitement as she kindly gave out autographs and genuine smiles to everyone. The energy and happiness in the air sparked a passion inside me, and I knew that performing was my calling. Even as a child, I longed for the day when I would walk out of that door and be greeted by cheering fans. The experience created a memory I will cherish forever.

I realize now how significant that moment was for me, not only because it solidified my desire to become a performing artist but because as a Black child I witnessed a Black cast on a Broadway stage. Experiencing that with my family is something I hope every child of color has the opportunity to do. It's important for children to see themselves in spaces where they typically aren't represented. This is crucial, as it can be incredibly inspiring and empowering. Seeing someone who looks like you in a nontraditional space can help instill the belief that you, too, can achieve your goals and pursue your dreams. I want to express my gratitude to the cast of the show that night for showing this little Black girl that her dreams of being part of a live Broadway cast as a performing artist could indeed come true.

My family when we first moved to Randolph

3

The Beginning or the End?

As our house was being built in Randolph, my parents decided to enroll us in private school. It was the fifth grade for me and the sixth grade for Cheryl. Pingry was—and still is—considered a top-tier private school in New Jersey. It was known for being very elite, predominantly white, and catering to privileged students. I had attended mostly Black schools until then, and the culture shock of attending not just a private school but one where people like us—Black and middle class—didn't quite fit in was significant. I find it intriguing that their website now promotes their commitment to diversity and inclusion, particularly considering my past experience was not reflective of those values.

During my first semester, there was a woodshop class, and I don't remember the instructor's name, but I can remember certain students receiving extra attention and praise. Make no mistake, I was not one of those students. Although a quiet child, I always did what I was told and performed well in my classes. We were given several options to make a woodshop project, and I decided on a

"Home Sweet Home" plaque. I had to cut the wood, trace the letters on it, then use a circular drill to impress the letters into the wood. I was only allowed to do three letters at a time, and since I wanted to do a good job, I took my time. Most of the kids were done with their pencil holders or jewelry boxes and had already moved on to shellacking their work to give it a polished feel, so I felt rushed. When I was done, I proceeded to add shellac as well. But the teacher came over to me and reprimanded me, saying that I had used so much, I could take a bath in it. The other kids started smirking, whispering, and pointing at me, and I immediately felt embarrassed. This was a fifth-grade shop class, so there was no reason for him to shame me instead of teaching me the correct way. For the rest of class, I simply kept my head down. That was the start of my feeling the need to blend in, to avoid standing out, and to dim my own light.

I'm not sure why I didn't tell my parents what happened that day, but I kept it to myself. So when our house was finally completed, I was ecstatic. We got to move, thus transferring schools again. We only stayed at Pingry for one year. My mom kept my "Home Sweet Home" plaque and hung it up in our new house, which was absolutely stunning. We were involved in every detail, choosing the countertops and lighting fixtures and selecting wallpaper for each room. While my parents picked out the furnishings, Cheryl and I got to pick out our room decor. We even got to have our own phone lines. We were over the moon.

The living room had sky-blue carpet with plush velvet couches that were a dark paisley and a love seat that matched. We had a black Wurlitzer Spinet piano with an oversized lounge chair on the side. It was one of my favorite rooms, although we rarely spent time in it. Across from this room was the foyer and the dining room, with a thick mahogany table where we sometimes ate dinner. My mother was a fine dishware collector, so we had a lavish display of plates that stretched across the length of the dining room. The TV room had French doors and a fireplace, another one of my favorites, mainly because that's where we spent the most time together as a family.

My father had a home office upstairs, which was convenient for running his business. Our house was surrounded by trees, offering him the quiet he needed to focus; I quickly learned what skunk cabbage was and became familiar with tadpoles and the sound of crickets. There was a long driveway that led up to the house, making it look like something out of a storybook. Four bedrooms, two and a half baths. It was very different from Hillside.

Upon settling into our home, my dad took care of the landscaping. We had a huge front lawn that sloped down to the house, and our backyard was almost completely wooded. I learned about the importance of landscaping from my dad and how much pride people put into making their homes look good on the outside.

There was a time when my father was working in front of our house and a car pulled up. The person inside asked him how much he would charge to do their lawn. This is why representation matters. When people don't see Black individuals in certain spaces, it perpetuates stereotypes, such as assuming that a Black man doing yard work in an upscale neighborhood couldn't possibly be taking care of his own lawn at his own home. He must be a gardener.

I made friends in school easily, and soon I moved from the

sixth grade into the seventh. Randolph grade schools combined middle and high school, so there were more kids changing classrooms and much harder work. I was a little nervous but up for the challenge. One of our neighbors had a big family and befriended us. I'd play with one of the sisters, and we'd go back and forth to each other's house. One day I was over there, and my friend's mom asked if I wanted a bagel. I said, "What's a bagel?" She guffawed and said, "Oh my God, you don't know what a bagel is? A bialy?" I shook my head, and they immediately gave me a bagel with butter. It was so good. The creaminess of the butter along with the saltiness of the bagel . . . I was in heaven. As soon as I got home, I asked my mom to get us some and was shocked that she knew exactly what they were.

In Hillside, the slang we used was different. We would say things like "honey chile" or "y'all." But in Randolph, they said "you guys" for everything, even if they were talking to girls. They consistently included a "g" at the end of their words as well. "Goin'" vs. "going," "lovin'" vs. "loving." I thought back to the first time I used "you guys" in a sentence instead of my usual slang. I felt so awkward and self-conscious, enunciating each syllable with care, almost as if I were in a competition for proper pronunciation. My new friends effortlessly maintained their accents and pronunciation; it was just how they normally talked. To my surprise, they didn't seem to notice my struggle with adjusting to their linguistic style. Despite how I talked, my friends embraced me for who I was.

As I look back, it was these lighthearted moments that made my integration into this vibrant community even more memorable. In the end, it showed me that fitting in isn't about flawless pronunciation, but rather embracing the unique qualities that make us who we are, even if that means stumbling over our words from time to time.

I was slowly finding my way and got along with just about everyone in the neighborhood. Which is why when a certain incident occurred outside our home, it surprised and somewhat scared me. I was just settling into bed when a car pulled into our driveway with its headlights on and started beeping the horn. *Beeeeep. Beeeeep. Beeeeep.* They honked their horn for about a minute, but it seemed like forever. It now reminds me of the Amazon horror series *Them*. I remember lying there in silence, afraid to move, hoping they would just go away. I felt like melting into my bed. As soon as they left, I jumped out of bed and ran downstairs and told my parents. They told me they hadn't heard anything and had been watching television in the TV room, which was located at the back of the house. I started to think that maybe I had imagined it all. Especially since nothing like that ever happened again.

///////

My mother found a dance school in Dover called Phil Grassia Dance School, where they taught various styles of dance. Phil was a vaudeville hoofer who taught tap. He was kind, caring, and patient, so I took private and semiprivate lessons with him. I studied under him for a couple years until he passed down his studio to one of his instructors, a woman named Chloe. She was fabulous and fully invested in the students. She would often take a few of us into Manhattan to do master classes. A master class is when a large ballroom is rented, and a prominent choreographer comes in to teach dance combinations. Master classes can be taught in jazz, tap, ballet, and many other styles. She wanted to give us a taste of what it was like to be a professional dancer in New York. This was the first time I was introduced to Frank Hatchett.

Frank was, and still is, a legend in the dance world. He was an extremely skilled dancer and choreographer who cofounded the Broadway Dance Center. He's best known for his mastery of jazz dance and worked with countless celebrities like Madonna, Janet Jackson, and Jennifer Lopez. Many of his techniques have been taught for generations, even after he passed away. He had a signature style called the VOP, where he encouraged students to accent or individualize their steps. Frank always believed that in order to be a great dancer, you had to *feel* the music, not just perform the moves.

I would spend the night at my nana's house on weekends when I had a master class. We enjoyed drinking tea with milk and sugar together at night and again in the morning before I departed. Chloe would collect each student in the morning for our journey into New York City. After teaching a full combination, Frank would break down the class into small groups so each group could perform. When class ended, we could talk with him and even get a picture. He was so approachable and loved to pass on his love of the arts.

Before heading back to Jersey, Chole would treat us to lunch and then take us home. It felt good to have Chole believe in me, and I was proud to attain these experiences at such a young age.

When I was about ten, my mother put me in my first beauty pageant, Little Miss Ebony. It felt like a hundred girls were there for the crown, although in reality, it was probably more like twenty-five. We underwent rehearsals weeks before the pageant, where we practiced an opening number and then prepared for the swimsuit, talent, and evening gown segments. On the night of the pageant, I arrived early to get ready for the event, which commenced around six o'clock. Due to the extensive duration of each section, the night felt prolonged. Furthermore, the added adrenaline had a draining effect on me. I found myself struggling to stay awake as the crowning ceremony unfolded. Ultimately, I secured the position of fourth runner-up. Upon hearing my name, I woke up and approached to collect my trophy, where I sensed my parents' immense pride in the audience. Participating in the pageant was a rewarding experience, distinct from my previous exposure to being onstage during the fourth-grade recital. I was genuinely pleased that I took part in it.

After the pageant, I moved my focus back to dance for the next few years. My mother made sure to come to every dance performance throughout my middle school, high school, and college career. My father was always busy making sure there was a roof over our heads, food on the table, and clothes on our backs, so he wasn't always able to come. But he made an effort to attend any performance he could, which I appreciated.

On Friday nights, my mother would have her weekly mahjongg game with her girlfriends, and all the kids would get together to watch *The Love Boat* or *The Dukes of Hazzard*. We would put Noxzema on our faces and play around, sometimes making it a sleepover. I loved nights like these and looked forward to them every week.

///////

One Saturday morning, my sisters and I were upstairs playing when my parents called us downstairs. I thought my father was making his famous weekend breakfast and that they wanted us to have a family talk. I was thinking, *Wow, we're finally going to Disneyland.* Or something to that effect, you know, like a trip. Something fun and exciting for our family, since they were making such a big deal about this announcement.

They just kept going back and forth between each other, and Cheryl and I thought it was a game. We started smiling and laughing, saying, "Tell us. Tell us."

"You tell them."

"No, you tell them."

And it went on like this for a good five minutes. Then my dad finally said, "Your mama and I are getting a divorce."

My heart stopped. I wasn't exactly sure what a divorce was, but I knew it wasn't good. As if that wasn't bad enough, we were told to get dressed to go help our father pick out furniture for his new apartment.

Apartment?

When had he had time to even look for a place? I remember standing there, trying to wrap my head around what was being told to us. The thought of not having my mom and dad together in the same home had never crossed my mind. My mom called my name to snap me out of my thoughts, and we were sent to our room to get dressed. Cheryl and I kept our emotions in check as we put on our clothes, then hurried back downstairs. Once we were ready to go, my mom kissed our cheeks and told us to be good and go with our father. We went to Wesco Dinette, a small furniture store on Route 10. I was in a trance as we walked through the store, picking out tables, couches, and accent furniture for his new place.

The whole time I kept thinking, *What is happening?* It felt like my family was being torn apart. Along with running the business and managing real estate acquisitions, my father had found himself diving into new entrepreneurial endeavors that required him to work long hours and travel frequently. He was passionately pursuing his ambitions, working tirelessly to achieve his goals. This often meant that he was not able to spend as much time at home as he had in the past. As a result, the dynamic of my parents' relationship had changed, with my mother shouldering more of the responsibilities at home while my father dedicated himself to his professional pursuits.

I wasn't sure if the divorce meant we would have to eventually sell our home, but I did know that I loved my room, loved our neighbors, and I didn't want to leave. Where would we go? My mind wandered as Cheryl and I walked around the furniture store in a daze.

///////

Once visitation was decided, we saw our dad often; he still maintained his office in our family home. Peaches was ten years younger than me, so she spent a lot more time with our father than Cheryl and I did. We were older now—me twelve, Cheryl thirteen—and wanted to hang with friends, go to parties, go roller-skating, or go to the new Rockaway mall. On weekends, Peaches would go to my dad's apartment or to visit our uncle Bobby and aunt Valerie while we hung out. We were each handling the divorce differently, just trying to feel safe in our own way.

When an opportunity presented itself to travel with my school to Germany, my parents let me go. I was taking a German class at the time, so my German teacher and her assistant traveled to Germany with about ten of us for two weeks. Most of the kids in our class were excited about the trip, but I felt a bit anxious, finding comfort in knowing that I was traveling with people I knew. We got to see all the museums, castles, tourist sites, restaurants, and, of course, practice our German. It was strange to me that our trip would be intertwined with high school students from another school, but it was. My first few days there were an adjustment. Many of the students snuck alcohol or boys into their rooms, which made me feel a little uncomfortable. I wasn't having as much fun as I thought I would and got tired of eating the same thing every night, schnitzel—a cutlet of veal pounded thin by a meat tenderizer, then dipped in flour, egg, and breadcrumbs—because that's the only thing on the menu I recognized.

One night I went to the teachers' room to tell them that I wanted to go home. This was the longest I'd spent away from my parents and sisters, and the distance was getting to me. My teacher and the assistant shared a room and told me to come inside. They poured me a glass of wine and told me to relax and that we'd only be there for a few more days. I felt weird, so I went back to my room.

The next morning, I wanted to go downstairs to the hotel lobby, where I could exchange some money for the day's excursion. The elevator door opened, and I asked if it was going down. I couldn't understand anyone, so I got on, hoping it was going in my direction. Instead, it went up. Rather than get off, I figured I'd just take the ride up, then go back down. As people filed off the elevator, I noticed an older gentleman from a foreign country standing toward the back. One by one, people got off the elevator until I was left alone with him. Once we were alone, he started talking to me in English, asking my name and where I was from. When I didn't respond, he moved closer to me, blocking the door. I moved to the back of the elevator, hoping he would get off soon.

Suddenly, he stepped closer to me and tried to kiss me. I immediately stiffened and stepped back into the corner of the elevator, but there wasn't much room. I pushed him and told him to get away from me, but now he was getting forceful. The elevator stopped on the top floor, and when the doors opened, he put his arms around me and tried to pull me off the elevator. I pushed and shoved with all my might, and as the doors were about to close, I grounded myself so he couldn't pull me out, and he let me go. I rushed to the panel of buttons to hit "door close." My heart raced as tears sprang to my eyes. Reaching the lobby, I went to the exchange counter as planned. My teacher could tell something was wrong, and I told her what had happened. A few of the high school boys overheard and ran to the elevators to look for the man but never found him. As I caught my breath, we waited in the lobby for the rest of the students to join us and continued on for the remainder of the trip. I made sure never to ride in an elevator alone for years, and he will be forever engrained in my mind.

Mom and her girls

4

Growing Pains

Even though Randolph was mostly white, I don't recall encountering a lot of racism personally. As a matter of fact, I made some amazing friends who made me feel welcome, many of whom I am still friends with today. Growing up biracial was normal for me. It's the only life I've ever known, having a white mother and a Black father. So I felt comfortable in both predominantly white and predominantly Black environments. There was really only one instance that I can think of when someone said something that outwardly offended me.

I was hanging out with one of my female friends, whose older brother had a party. The topic of Martin Luther King Jr. came up. It was early January 1983, and his birthday was right around the corner. There was a lot of controversy because the White House had just announced that it would become a federal holiday. I remember her brother tensing up and getting angry at the topic, stating that MLK Day wasn't a real holiday. In fact, it was a "nigger holiday," and he would never take off to observe it. Everyone immediately looked at me, and I was standing there like, *What did he just say?* I couldn't believe he could be so callous and uncaring about someone who fought and lost their life for civil rights, especially as his sister's very Black friend stood there. I couldn't even find the words to express my anger at his ignorant statement, so I just walked out of the room.

Thankfully, I didn't have to be around him much, and his sister and other family members never expressed that kind of racist thinking. That was an unnerving and uncomfortable scenario to be in. I quickly understood that it was important for me to remain grounded and not let others influence me.

As I was nearing the end of my freshman year of high school, there was a lot of talk about college. Most of my friends had no qualms about what they would be doing after graduation, especially the girls. It seemed as if their lives had already been mapped out.

Go to college. Earn a degree. Fall in love. Get married.

It was a no-brainer for them. Yet I wasn't sure what I wanted to do. When asked about my plans, I'd just keep my answers vague or remain silent. Although I loved to dance, I wasn't sure if it was something I could pursue professionally. The Broadway show I'd seen so many years ago didn't happen as often as I would have liked, so that dream felt a bit far-fetched. Not to mention, I was still processing how to live without having both my parents in the same home. Though my dad came around often and would take us out to brunch or dinner, it wasn't the same as all of us living in one place.

Dad's sewer cleaning business was going strong, and despite the separation, Mom continued assisting by answering the phones while also working to attain her real estate license. There was tension one morning when my father came over to the house to check his messages and service calls. Cheryl had already left for school, and I was downstairs making breakfast when my parents started arguing about custody. Peaches was still quite young, and my mother vehemently expressed that she wouldn't allow my father to take us. This led to my father getting angry and yelling, "I'm going to get custody. There's no way I'm going to let you raise them to be like you."

I recall having a strong desire to grab a frying pan and hurl it against the wall just to put an end to their argument. Instead, I concentrated on preparing my breakfast as they continued to bicker loudly. When I returned home from school that day, I went upstairs and began jumping up and down at the top of the stairs. I was filled with so much pent-up frustration, it threatened to overtake me from the inside out. My mother scolded me to stop. "Jennifer, stop it right now! You're acting like a two-year-old." But I completely tuned her out, unwilling to hear anything she had to say. If only she could understand how angry and hurt I was. The yelling became overwhelming. I needed an outlet for those bottled-up emotions I was carrying around. What was I meant to do with those feelings? Was I expected to act as if nothing had occurred, as though I were unaffected?

I was affected, and I was tired. I simply wanted the arguing to end.

///////

Between my freshman and sophomore years of high school, my dad took my sisters and me to Hawaii. We stayed in a hotel right across the street from the beach. It was warm, everyone was friendly, and I had rice and pineapple each morning for breakfast. I think he was really trying to bond with us. Be a family, make memories. Upon returning, I don't think my dad was genuinely happy. He really loved Mom and us, and I could tell he missed his family.

By the end of sophomore year, I stopped dancing altogether. With everything going on with my parents, my focus had dropped to zero. I'd lost my excitement for dance and was only interested in hanging out with friends.

Often we would go roller-skating, and somebody from our group would get a bottle of Boone's Farm wine. We would drink behind the roller rink, then head inside and grab food, go skating, and have a good time. I had also started experimenting with marijuana, and I enjoyed getting high from time to time, letting my problems float away with the smoke.

Boys were another welcome distraction. I had learned how to style my hair and do my makeup from taking classes at a modeling agency in Madison, New Jersey. There was an older guy named Mark, who was cool with my guy friends, so he was always around. He provided the alcohol, and before long, our conversations and playful glances evolved into something more, and we started dating. In hindsight, I wonder why a twenty-four-year-old man would be interested in a seventeen-year-old girl, but at the time, it didn't seem like that big of a deal. My group of friends had become my family.

As Mark and I grew closer, he expressed his desire to marry me and purchase a spacious home in Pennsylvania where we could start a family. It sounded appealing, although I hadn't yet determined my own aspirations for the future. His vision did offer comfort and stability.

However, our circumstances would soon change.

I was at Mark's place one afternoon, leisurely enjoying a Kahlúa and milk while watching music videos on the newly introduced MTV channel. Suddenly, the song "Legs" by ZZ Top began playing. I was captivated by the song and got up and started dancing.

The video featured numerous stunning women in various settings, showcasing their long, beautiful legs. They were exiting cars, trying on clothes in stores, strolling around, and flaunting their charm. I was fascinated, though I couldn't discern Mark's thoughts as he busied himself with straightening up the living room. I exclaimed, "I would love to be in a music video," before a broad smile adorned my face. The video had me completely entranced.

"Oh, come on, you could never do that," Mark scoffed, and then chuckled as he left the room. His response caught me off guard. I was sincere in my desire to be a part of a music video, and his reaction made it clear that he did not support me or my ambitions.

That marked the beginning of the end for us. I became withdrawn and distant from him, and before long, our relationship disintegrated entirely. I just couldn't get past his hurtful words regarding something I was passionate about.

One Saturday, my sister and I were excited about going roller-skating with friends, our usual weekend activity. Unfortunately, it turned out to be my dad's turn to take us out for dinner. We were visibly irritated, as teenagers often are. Who would prefer spending time with their father and having a dull dinner over enjoying themselves at the skating rink? Despite our disappointment, we reluctantly went with him. Our friends assured us they would wait for us to return.

At the Randolph Diner, we sat in almost complete silence, simply wanting to finish the meal. We got excited once my dad paid the check, and told him our friends were eagerly waiting for us at the skating rink. Finally getting into the car, we felt relieved to be heading home. I was in the front seat, my two sisters in the back. Cheryl and I had agreed she would take the front seat on the way to the rink, and I would have it going back. This was an understanding between siblings, with no room for stops in between. Consequently, Peaches had no choice but to sit in the back, as she was the youngest. But then my dad unexpectedly missed the street he was supposed to turn down. When I pointed out that he had missed the turn, he casually said, "I'm not taking you home."

Pleading with him, I begged, "Come on, Dad. Our friends are waiting for us." He revealed that our grandpa was coming to town, requiring us to go to the airport to pick him up. Rather than address my constant pleading, my dad began hurriedly searching his vehicle, car swerving on the road. I knew what he kept hidden in his glove box, and everything within me froze. Tears welled up in my eyes instantly as I began apologizing for whatever wrongdoing I had committed. I internalized his threatening behavior, wrongly believing his actions to be my fault. "I'm sorry, I'm so sorry." Meanwhile, Cheryl and Peaches held each other in the back seat. He stopped his "search" and continued driving. I turned my gaze toward the windshield and remained silent.

As soon as we got home, we told my mother what had happened. I'm not sure why, but she never took anything my father did seriously. She always brushed him off and felt like he was just being dramatic. All bark and no bite. Some people might say that's crazy. But I guess she saw something in him that most people didn't. He was struggling and hurting.

////////

Now that my parents' divorce was finalized, my mom began dating. It was a bit strange for me at first, but I understood that she was trying to move on with her life. I didn't feel upset about it, but was curious as to the kind of guys she was interested in. I only wanted her to be happy. This was sometimes made difficult, since my father would come over to the house unannounced to access his home office or see us. Honestly, I feel like he was secretly keeping an eye on her.

There was this one guy named Scooter, someone she had known since grade school. He was the first guy she took seriously after my dad. My mom had liked him back in the day because he was a nice guy. One particular afternoon, my friend Gina, who lived right next door, was over at our house. When my father came over, he noticed Scooter's car in the driveway. The first question he asked upon walking in the door was "Whose car is that?"

Meanwhile, Scooter was sitting in the living room, sweating and shaking profusely. He was deathly afraid of my father. Noticing Scooter's discomfort, Gina asked if he wanted to go over to her house to wait for my father to leave. He agreed, and we quickly retreated next door. Gina's grandmother MoMo, who was from Tulsa, Oklahoma, always had her gray hair in curlers and fingernails painted white. She was smoking a cigarette in some patterned muumuu, talking up a storm. Gina and I got a kick out of the situation, and so did her grandmother. MoMo loved Scooter's company and kept him entertained while he waited.

Unfortunately, despite how happy Scooter made my mom, he didn't last very long. I thought for sure Mom would stop dating after that, but to my surprise, she never let my dad stop her from finding happiness elsewhere. As for my dad's antics, I could see that he was also trying to navigate the changes in his own way. He, too, began dating.

By my senior year of high school, I was in a program where I went to school half a day, then worked for the other half. During my off-time, I continued hanging out with friends. My mom and dad weren't too involved with my college decisions. Dad had only gone to college for one semester, and Mom hadn't gone at all. It was different for us, for our generation. High school guidance counselors had a bigger role in assisting students with their options for continuing education. Cheryl had already taken her PSATs and SATs and was enrolled at Pace University. I was not looking forward to those exams. I never understood the need for standardized testing and never thought it was a true reflection of a student's abilities, but I had no choice.

Now that I wasn't dancing, I had to find something else to do. Nothing felt like a fit. The only thing I'd ever been passionate about besides my family was dance. Realizing this, I made the decision to get myself back into it and attend a dance school. I took the SATs, did some research, and found that Glassboro State College had a great dance program. Even though I was a little late in making this decision, I was determined to begin the application process and start my journey toward getting back to doing what I loved.

I was determined to make my parents proud.

When I arrived at my high school guidance counselor's office and shared my enthusiasm for attending Glassboro State, instead of supporting and aiding me in my endeavors, she chuckled, then looked at me and said, "Jennifer, you're not ready for college."

Tap dance recital at Phil Grassia's studio

5

Falling Hard and Falling Fast

Could my race have had something to do with that guidance counselor's response? I don't know, but the thought did cross my mind. She directed me to apply to the County College of Morris, located right in Randolph, stating that I wasn't ready for a four-year college. Her advice made me reconsider my plans. I often wonder how life would have turned out had I gone to my first choice. But I believe everything happens for a reason, even if it seems negative at first. The counselor's words guided me to a path that turned out to be meaningful and important. While my peers were packing up and going cross-country, I was putting the pieces together. Not knowing what else to do, I went to register for classes.

I initially picked a business major, thinking it would offer flexibility. I thought being a business major would prepare me to open a studio one day. I didn't realize that dance was a major at CCM. However, after discovering the college had a modern dance company named Beyond the NJ Turnpike and offered dance as a major, I switched from business to dance. There I met some wonderful people and learned modern dance. It was new and refreshing, strengthening me while I learned different ways to move my body. I started to hone my technique. Everyone in the school was extremely talented. We had performances at the CCM theater, and we partook in an outreach program teaching movement to blind children. It was wonderful to see them move freely and uninhibitedly in the open space.

There was a lot to balance during my first semester. Making time for my classes and schoolwork, then trying to learn a new dance form and prepare for performances was taking its toll. After a show, my mother told me that if I wanted to truly dance, I had to go to New York, as that's where all the great dance schools and programs were located. We got into her car, and she took me to Manhattan to look at studios. During the ride, I remember thinking that I was finally on my way to my future. I planned to get focused, take dance seriously again, and find my footing in the world.

We went to three dance schools: Steps, Alvin Ailey, and the Broadway Dance Center. Both Steps and the Broadway Dance Center had classes that you could sign up and pay for. You didn't have to audition or need a recommendation to get into the school. Alvin Ailey, however, would require an audition, and if I made it in, I'd join their dance company. I couldn't see myself in a company setting much like the college dance company—I wanted music videos and theater. The Broadway Dance Center was where I really felt at home. Especially since Frank Hatchett was there. I loved his style and wanted to take his classes again.

I started with beginner's jazz and became a regular at the studio, where I made friends. I would sit by the window or door to watch

Frank's advanced class, determined to make it in one day. Frank would notice me and eventually became my mentor. His mentorship and guidance proved to be fundamental to my career.

I frequently traveled between CCM and NYC, adding an additional level of dedication and a hectic schedule. One of the classes I took at BDC, a ballet class, was with famed instructor Peff Modelski, who had the most striking ballet turnout I had ever seen. I really wanted to nail down that first and fifth position, pointing my toes like some of the dancers who had elegant arches. My feet were somewhat flat, so I was constantly working on the arch of my foot and stretching—you always wanted to be able to stretch farther, stretch more. If I wasn't working on my stretches, I was working on my turns. Turning was a big thing for me. Some people could just twirl for days, but me, I struggled. Peff would keep pushing me, giving me exercises that helped. One was to place a heavy can in my right hand with my arm extended while turning. The idea was that the momentum from the can would pull me effortlessly in the appropriate direction, helping me to balance my weight to get the right amount of speed to complete the turn. To my surprise, it worked. And eventually, I got rid of the can and turned on my own.

My day-to-day schedule went something like this: I would have an early morning class at CCM, then head straight to Frank's eleven o'clock intermediate class—I had moved up from beginner—then Peff's class in the afternoon. In between, I'd run to the deli across the street to get some kind of fruit or toast and iced coffee, then get right back into it. I'd wrap up my day after five with a few more classes to complete my full-time schedule. I'd often take two or three dance classes a day, interspersed between my regular college classes. Every time my father handed me money for the trains and classes each morning, I felt like he thought I wasn't contributing and that my dancing was more like a wish on a star. Like I was living in a fantasy world. After all, my father is a self-made man.

Our routine consisted of him picking me up after my class at CCM each morning on his way to work and taking me to the train station. He'd give me twenty dollars, and I would ride the train into the city. I'd spend all day there, and then I would come home and perform the combinations I had learned for my mother. I finally felt like I was getting back to myself. To the old Jennifer. The happy little girl who loved to dance. I was making strides in my classes, becoming a better dancer, and the people there . . . I just felt so comfortable around them. We would practice together and encourage one another. We shared a common interest and love for the arts. A way of expressing yourself through your own body.

BDC was located in Midtown and had convenient commuting options. During that time, Times Square was quite different from its current state. Nowadays it is considered kid-friendly, but back then it was not as much.

After returning home from Frank's class one evening, I was showing my mother the routine I'd just learned, and she looked at me stone-faced and said, "Jennifer, what are you doing with your life?"

Her tone and words made me pause.

I could see the look of worry on her face. The question took me by surprise because I felt like I was getting really good. Couldn't she see how much I wanted to make a career out of dance? I wanted to be on Broadway like Stephanie Mills and walk out of that magical backstage door. I wanted the lights, costumes, and applause.

I went back to my room to seriously consider her question. I got scared . . . nervous.

What *was* I doing with my life?

Could I really become a Broadway star like Stephanie Mills?

Despite my concerns, I got out of bed the following day and headed to CCM and then to BDC. It was a familiar routine for me, and I felt at ease with it, even though I was unsure of where it would take me in life. No, I may not have had a solid step-by-step plan, but I knew that if I continued to work hard and master my craft, I could see myself dancing on a grand stage.

Not long after that, as my father took me to the train station, he said, "Jenn . . . this is the last time I'm doing this here."

"Doing what?" I asked.

But he only stared at me, and I knew what he meant. This would be the last time he would drop me off at the train station and give me his hard-earned twenty dollars to pay for my day at dance school. I was devastated. Dance was such an integral part of my being. I loved the music and moving my body to a count of eight. The sharpness or softness of a step. The way in which a feeling or thought could be conveyed by movement. It was all enchanting. I was in New York City, studying under the world-renowned Frank Hatchett. I had to find a way to continue; otherwise, I'd have to stop dancing altogether.

As my parents continued to navigate the tumultuous waters of their divorce, they were also grappling with the complexities of moving forward as individuals and co-parents to three young girls while living in separate households. Although Cheryl and I were considered adults, empowered to forge our own paths, we were still young, so of course as young people we made mistakes.

I couldn't focus on going back to school while juggling the commitments of dance. I had to find a job and figure out how to move to New York, where there were countless opportunities. I still lived at home with my mom and didn't have the money to move out on my own. My parents wanted me to have a stable income, instead of relying on them financially, so my hope was to line up an evening job so I could keep dancing and go to auditions during the day.

There was a cheery and social girl named Ashley who frequented Broadway shows and spent time at the backstage door, getting to know the actors. I had met her in Frank's class. Although she didn't have a typical dancer's body, she defied stereotypes and excelled at VOP. She mentioned wanting to introduce me to someone and brought me to see a Broadway musical directed by Michael Bennett in the heart of the Broadway district, Shubert Alley. The show gave us a glimpse into the lives of performers and choreographers. Walking through the famous alley, the magical atmosphere reminded me of limitless possibilities and gave me chills. That's where she introduced me to a man named Christopher. He asked me out, and we planned to meet at Tony Roma's shortly after.

Chris was a performer on Broadway and a vocalist. He took an immediate liking to me, and our friendship quickly blossomed into something more. He was tall, standing well over six feet, lean, and had beautiful brown skin. A decade older than me, he was charming and assured me that he would guide me through the intricacies of the industry. We enjoyed each other's company, and I began to spend more time with him.

Chris had performed in several major Broadway shows, including *Starlight Express*. *Starlight Express* was a 1984 British musical about a child's train set that came to life and all the obstacles the steam car faced on his journey to becoming the fastest engine while winning the heart of his first love, Pearl. Chris introduced me to his agent, who gave me tips on auditioning and the business as a whole.

Soon I was spending nights at his place and then he gave me a key. It was much easier to hop a train downtown to take my dance classes than to travel from New Jersey. I spoke to my mother as often as I could, though my relationship with my father had trailed off. Since there were no cell phones, I'd usually call her from the apartment on the landline.

Chris's apartment was right in the heart of uptown, on 188th Street in Washington Heights. Staying with him allowed me to get a feel of what it was like living the Broadway dream, working in the business. He was always giving me pointers and teaching me acting, singing, and dance techniques. There was a mirror and ballet barre in his apartment, so I could practice at night, especially when he wasn't around. Then I'd wait up for him to come home, and he'd tell me about his day. He usually brought sandwiches from the local deli, and we'd relax on the sofa and watch David Letterman. As Chris spoke, I was in awe of him. He represented everything I wanted for myself, and I knew if I kept going, my dreams were within my grasp. The more I heard him speak, the more I knew I wanted that life. A short time later, I had an opportunity to dance on *Club MTV*.

Starlight Express was in need of replacements and understudies, so we thought it would be a great opportunity for me to audition. I practiced my skating abilities with Ashley, and although we fell quite a bit, I persisted. On audition day, the skating portion came first.

Practice and my experience from my high school days at Roller World paid off, and I was selected for the singing part. It's important to note that I was new to reading sheet music and still learning, but Chris had shared the sheet music for "Walking on Sunshine" with me. Even though I was prepared, nerves got the best of me, and I sang off-key throughout the entire song. The casting director and show managers wanted to laugh but politely held back until I left and was out of earshot. When Chris returned home, he was like, "Yeah, the singing part, we need to work on that."

We shared a laugh, and I practiced my melodies.

I wasn't getting much money from the gigs I secured, and Chris wanted me to contribute more to the household. I continued looking for a job that would allow me to audition and take classes during the day and work at night. I had been auditioning without procuring stable employment. A dance gig here, a modeling job there, but nothing that provided substantial income for me to afford my own place. It made me wonder if my parents were right. Should I perhaps scale back my ambitions and settle into a nine-to-five job at a company that offered benefits?

Finally, I landed a position as a telemarketer in the evenings, working from six to eleven. It wasn't difficult work, but it definitely wasn't my true calling. I primarily contacted older individuals and tried to persuade them to add a rider to their insurance plan. Due to starting work at six, I would make calls well into dinnertime, family time, and late into the evening, often prompting serious attitudes, along with the question "Do you know what time it is?"

I couldn't help but think about my fellow dancers who were working as bartenders, servers, and busboys. I realized this was a part of the industry that many people don't see. Expressing our emotions and feelings through dance and movement doesn't always pay the bills. Even though I wasn't pursuing what truly resonated with my soul, I understood that sacrifices needed to be made in order to remain in the industry.

Chris's and my relationship began to decline gradually. Our interactions were limited, as I would aim to go to bed before he returned home or leave early in the morning for dance class and then work. When we did communicate, it would often escalate into an argument. I disliked engaging in conflicts with him or anyone else, and once again I found myself questioning if I was on the right path. What message was the universe trying to convey? I had to seriously contemplate what I was doing. While my high school friends appeared to be thriving by pursuing degrees, I was here with nothing.

////////

Chris mentioned to me that he would be meeting up with his previous partner, Margo. She was also a performer and had come to town to perform in a show. Since he rarely mentioned her, I assumed they had lost touch. He said they were going out for dinner, and considering their past, I wasn't worried. I even wished him a pleasant evening as he left. However, I started to regret that decision when he called later to inform me that he wouldn't be coming home. He said he'd be staying at a hotel because he felt I wasn't offering enough support, and he needed some time away. I was surprised by his response but figured I would let him cool off, and we could talk things over when he returned in the morning refreshed.

Maybe he would miss me and recognize his mistake—want to make peace and work it out.

The next morning, I heard him come in through the door and put down his keys. He came into the bedroom and sat on the edge of the bed. I had my back to him, waiting to see what he was going to say. He started talking, and, having just woken up, I wasn't responding as quickly as he would have liked. I turned to give him my attention, but when his tone got nastier, I rolled over, facing away from him because I didn't want to fight. This must have agitated him further, because he got very close to me and poked me in the face, hard enough to leave a mark. I was nervous things might escalate, but he got up, left the room, and took his dog, Lulu, out.

I just sat there and cried. I only wanted things to get better. For us to work it out and get back to the fun couple we were in the beginning.

We didn't speak about Margo again.

With the incident behind us, I fell into a routine of going to dance class, heading downtown to my telemarketing job, and leaving at eleven to go home. I was getting used to the subway system by now, which trains to take where, and felt more comfortable riding them at different hours. The key to it was looking confident during your travels and remaining alert. I would always keep an eye out just in case I needed to act fast. My backup plan was that if anyone ever accosted me, I would act crazy. Like jumping up and down on the seat, mooing like a cow, or screaming out random names and phrases.

Luckily, I never had to implement these scare tactics.

At the 188th Street station, you had to take an elevator up to the street level, then walk out of a tunnel to get to the street. There would be people hanging out, and I never felt totally comfortable walking through there, but at least I was among other people who got off at the stop with me, so I was never alone. It was a busy station.

A moment sticks out to me when, after work, a young man stood at the tunnel's edge. I glanced over, and our eyes met. I can't explain it, but I got a sinking sensation in my gut. Frightened, I hurried home, almost running the remaining half block to Chris's apartment building. As I approached the outside door, I fumbled for the right key to gain entry and safety from this man. Seconds felt like minutes until I yanked the keys out of my purse and into the lock on the door. Securely inside the building, I closed the door behind me. As I walked toward the second door, I saw the man standing right outside. He gestured for me to let him in, but I shook my head as I waited for the elevator. The man began pressing all the apartment doorbells to gain entry while my heart raced. If he continued, someone would eventually buzz him in. Chris's building had an old, rickety elevator, so it took forever for it to get to the ground floor. When I stepped onto the elevator, the man screamed at me and banged on the door, demanding to be let inside. I pressed the button for Chris's floor hard and fast, fearing what might happen if he got in.

Just get me into the apartment was the only thought running through my mind.

Once I reached Chris's floor, I keyed into the apartment and locked the door. I slid down to the floor, trying to catch my breath as tears flowed freely down my cheeks. I knew I couldn't keep putting myself in situations like this. I had to find another way.

///////

Things started looking up when I learned about an audition for an upcoming music video. I was excited to try out and was over the moon when I landed the part. There were a slew of pretty ladies at the audition, and once we completed the choreography, the production team did a cut. This meant they let some dancers go. I was kept, and we continued to audition by learning another dance routine. Afterward I was asked about my availability. I stated I was available and was hired right there on the spot. I was learning how auditions worked and could tell when there was interest.

Heading home from that audition made me think of my old boyfriend's comments about me never making it into a music video. Well, eat your heart out, Mark. Not only did I kill it at the audition but I was the only Black woman cast for the shoot. The song "Infidelity" was by a group called Simply Red. The entire video was filmed in a subway station and one subway car. The choreography was pretty simple, so it didn't take me long to learn the moves. It was just a little awkward at first because of the difference in dance styles from stage to film. I also learned that filming is different from live performances and requires multiple takes, different angles, and new ideas that the director would like to try. Even though it was a long night—due to the star and a dancer disappearing for hours—I was excited to be a part of the video and couldn't wait to see myself on MTV.

After filming wrapped, several cast and crew members opted to hail a cab to return to Manhattan. Considering it was 1:00 a.m. and the shoot took place in Brooklyn, this seemed like the most practical choice. I was still elated, high on the fact that I had just shot my first music video, so getting home was the least of my concerns.

About five or six of us piled into a cab, and the driver looked very similar to the man who had cornered me on that elevator in Germany. Immediately the hairs on my arms stood up. His presence struck a chord in me. I tried to avoid letting my fears get the best of me and focused on chatting with the cast. One by one, each person got out of the car as we made our way to 188th Street, my stop. When the last guy got out, he gave me this look that I couldn't quite place. Everyone was giving me money since I would be the last person to get out, so I thought maybe he was worried there wouldn't be enough. I was new to this and wasn't really sure how to calculate everything. I just hoped I had enough money to pay the driver at the end of the trip.

En route to my apartment, we approached a long bridge near 125th Street that would lead uptown toward the Bronx. The bridge was closed off at this time, causing me to wonder why the driver was heading in that direction. I contemplated the possibility of an alternate route that I might be unaware of on the other side of the bridge. Sensing an unsettling feeling as we neared the entrance to the bridge, I slowly moved toward the door and grabbed my bag as the cab pulled into a cul-de-sac surrounded by derelict buildings. When the driver reached for the gear shift—I assumed to put the car in park—I seized the moment and leaped out while the car slowed to a stop. I sprinted down the pedestrian walkway of the bridge.

Turning the corner, I found myself standing on that bridge and quickly contemplated leaping off, anything to get me away from that man. I had no idea what he intended to do, but I didn't want to hang around to find out. In that terrifying moment, my mother's words echoed in my mind: "Jennifer, what are you doing with your life?" Peering over the railing, all I saw was pavement, and I hesitated to risk my life. I turned to prayer, beseeching God for a miracle to extricate me from this perilous situation.

As if God had heard me, I caught sight of another car's headlights, which snapped me back to reality, and I ran toward the entrance of the bridge. I jumped out into the middle of the street and began waving my arms in front of the car, asking the person to stop. The driver probably thought I was crazy for being on that deserted bridge in the first place, and he drove right past me.

With only one way out, I knew he'd have to turn around and come back in my direction. So I stood there and watched his rear lights dim, then noticed the taxi coming back my way. By this time, the driver of the car realized he had to turn around, too, and proceeded to make a U-turn. The cab stopped, and the other car pulled up alongside it. I ran to the other guy's car, and he had his window down. I grabbed onto the doorframe and told him how scared I was and asked him for a ride. The cabdriver looked at the guy and said, "Don't believe her. She just doesn't want to pay. She doesn't have enough money." The man told me I could take the driver's badge number and report him if needed. There were no cell phones, so I couldn't take a picture, and I didn't have a pen or paper on me. The guy told me that it would be okay to return to the cab and to trust him. I got back inside and made it to the apartment exhausted, relieved, and spent. I just wanted to sleep. I always wondered if the guy followed the cab to make sure I made it home safely.

Chris was awake when I stepped inside the apartment and

didn't like that I was coming in so late even though he knew I had been working. I tried explaining the whole ordeal with the cab-driver and that I wanted to go to bed. Things escalated between us, and in order to avoid another altercation, I pulled the phone into the bathroom and closed myself inside. As he screamed at me to open the door while banging on it, I called one of my friends from Frank's class. I told her what had happened and how scared I was. She encouraged me to reach out to my mother for help, but I was afraid of what she might say. The next thing I knew, Chris had disconnected the phone.

I stayed in the bathroom, in the tub, the farthest place from the door, until he quieted down, and I smelled the potent fumes of a joint. When all was silent, I eased out of the bathroom and out of the apartment to the nearest pay phone on the street. I called my mom crying and asked her to come and get me. My mom came immediately and picked me up from right where I stood.

Chris and I were over.

My dad took me to Chris's apartment a few days later so that I could get my stuff, and I moved back to New Jersey with my mom. My parents never asked me what happened that night, and we never spoke about it. My focus now was on taking matters into my own hands, using the skills I had learned to get me to the next level of my life and career.

And I would do it on my own.

JENNIFER JONES, 20, KICKS DOWN COLOR BARRIER

Ebony joins ivory
on Rockettes line

By HEIDI EVANS
Daily News Staff Writer

Eighty-eight world-class legs. And for the first time in the Rockettes' 62-year history, a pair of them will be black.

They belong to Jennifer Jones, a young dancer who on Jan. 31 will break the chorus line's color barrier when she struts her stuff with the others during the Super Bowl Sunday halftime show.

"When I heard on the news that the Rockettes were about to have (their) first black dancer, I didn't think it was me. I was so shocked," said Jones, flashing her large brown eyes.

"I'm glad it is me," she hastened to add.

sey Turnpike" and appeared in a few MTV videos.

The 5-foot-7 beauty found her way to Radio City after the Rockettes—under new management since 1979—encouraged minority dancers to audition last October.

Luckily for Jones, the Rockettes need extra legs—88 instead of the traditional 72—for the Super Bowl 88 formation. And so she was chosen.

"My friends told me I had the look," said Jones, who can do tap, jazz, ballet—and even 20 high kicks in a row without so much as an "ouch." Neither she nor her friends ever had seen the Rockettes, Jones noted, so she had no idea that the "look" had been all white.

sion, which is the hallmark of the Rockettes."

Jones said that when she was introduced to Holmes last week, the director claimed she had been misquoted. But Jones said she did not know what Holmes was talking about—she had not seen the article.

"She was very nice," Jones said of Holmes. The new Rockette said she does not expect to encounter any racism among the dancers and looks forward to being part of the dancing team.

Eileen Collins, a Rockette for 16 years, said she is looking forward to having Jones in the line.

"I think it's terrific. She is a gorgeous woman—I hate her for that reason," Col...

Daily News headline about my becoming a Rockette

6

If at First You Don't Succeed, Try, Try Again

oving in with my mom was a godsend. It allowed me to get back on my feet and establish a new routine. Additionally, it was a nice way to reconnect with my younger sister, Mom, and high school friends. I had made great strides in my budding career, so there was nothing to be ashamed of. I was now in a nationally syndicated music video, had made lots of connections in the business, and was making my own money at my telemarketing job. I felt enthusiastic about what came next and was still committed to dancing and Broadway stardom but accepted that it would have to take place from New Jersey.

In the spring of 1987, just before Chris and I separated, there was an audition listed in *Backstage* for the Rockettes. *Backstage* was a magazine that catalogued classes and auditions for Broadway shows, off-Broadway shows, musicals, music videos, acting classes, TV productions, etc. Initially, when I noticed the Rockettes audition, I bypassed it. I didn't know who they were, and I was focused on being a Broadway star. Then one of the girls in my dance class encouraged me to try out. She said, "Jennifer, you'd make a perfect Rockette; you should go."

She continued to tell me about who the Rockettes were and what they did at Radio City Music Hall. Upon reading the ad more thoroughly, I saw that ethnic minorities were encouraged to attend.

I woke up the morning of the audition and went back and forth with myself until finally I said, *What the heck? What do I have to lose?* I could still use some practice with auditions, so I figured this could help me get over my nerves.

Back then there was no internet. No Google or other search engines to quickly look something up to validate something's existence. I had to trust the word of my colleague. The audition was held at Radio City Music Hall in Midtown Manhattan, and the line of girls waiting to try out stretched for blocks around the Hall. Auditions started around ten o'clock in the morning, and that's the time I arrived. Looking at all the gorgeous women in their well-thought-out clothes, hair, and makeup, I considered leaving a couple times because I figured they were never going to hire me. There were a few times I even thought that if I left right then, I could still make it to Frank's eleven o'clock jazz class. But just as I got ready to leave, a voice inside me said, "Stay." And so I did.

Finally, after a couple hours of creeping toward the main entrance, I was greeted by Neil Conrad, the stage manager. He took the next twenty-five of us waiting in line inside the building. Intimidation intertwined with nerves crept in as we rode the elevator up to a small rehearsal hall where we could warm up. When I arrived in the room, fear consumed me as I watched the other girls stretching, kicking, and turning—they looked flawless. From their costume-like outfits to their hair and makeup, everything about them was spot-on glam. I wore my basic white leotard with black polka dots, leg warmers, and skin tone tights. I hadn't used any makeup, and my hair was pulled back in a simple ponytail. At BDC I learned you had to dress nice for auditions, so I had carefully planned my audition clothes, but I was still learning how to pull it together like the others had. I looked around the room and continued to take mental notes.

Each group was given a comp card to fill out with our name, phone number, weight, height, and contact information. After a few minutes of warming up and low chatter among the women, Neil Conrad came back into the room. He told us that he would call our names, and once called, we'd have to provide the comp card with our headshot and resume, tap shoes in hand, then line up in the order that he called us. I stood there feeling extremely unprepared. Not only did I not have my tap shoes but I also didn't have a headshot or resume. All I had was the comp card they had given to us.

Lesson learned.

After lining up, we walked into a large rehearsal hall and placed our belongings at the back of the room, then continued walking to the other side, where they had a person measuring our heights. The first order of business was making sure each girl was tall enough to make the line. I felt as if the people behind the desk were watching me. I wasn't sure why but figured it was just a part of the process. Still, I could feel my face getting flushed. I'm sure I was beet red.

Once I made the height requirement, I put on my character shoes and awaited instructions. There were about fifteen people from management behind a long table, as well as the Rockettes' pianist and Barbara, the Rockette captain. In the audition room, Violet Holmes introduced herself and told us she was going to teach us a tap combination. I was a little surprised because Violet was a short, stout woman with a pixie haircut. She was wearing high-water jazz pants, a Rockettes sweatshirt, ankle socks, and black flat tap shoes. I would later learn that she was one of Russell Markert's favorite dancers, so when he retired, he passed the line to her. You'd never know she was a world-renowned choreographer based on her appearance, but she could tap her butt off and excelled at choreographing gorgeous Rockette formations.

Violet was all business and extremely skilled, which taught me another important lesson: never judge a dancer by their appearance, as their performance could prove to be extraordinary.

She immediately began working the tap portion of the routine and had a unique way of teaching. I was used to using the "five, six, seven, eight" count to learn steps. Instead, she taught using an off melody of "beedle le de, beedle le da, da da." I was told every choreographer was different, and part of becoming a professional dancer was to adapt to each teacher. I learned the combination as best I could.

She then broke us up into groups of four: two in the front, two in the back. We did the combination and then changed lines, placing the two girls from the back in the front and so forth until everyone had a chance to go. We were taught another routine afterward because they were also casting for the Chita Rivera *Can-*

Can tour. We had to show our high-energy dance with cancan kicks and more. This included executing twenty of the iconic Rockette eye-high kicks. Once each of us had a turn, they thanked us for our time and told us they'd be in touch only if we were being considered for a callback.

Relieved that this part of the process was over, I walked to the back of the room to gather my belongings. Suddenly, I felt a tap on my shoulder. It was Neil Conrad. He said, "Jennifer, we're going to give you a callback. Make sure to bring your tap shoes, picture, and resume." I couldn't believe it. The idea that I might have the chance to work in that large rehearsal hall with floor-to-ceiling mirrors and gorgeous floor markings was beyond belief.

I was so excited about my audition, I didn't go to afternoon classes that day. Rather, I rushed back to New Jersey to get my things together—an old high school modeling headshot and a short resume that I had to get printed at Kinkos, plus my good tap shoes. I practiced the routine I learned just in case she taught the same one; it's always good to become familiar with the choreography.

Two days later, I got the call!

When I arrived, there was another Black woman in attendance, who was super talented and already working on Broadway. Even though I was nervous, I knew I had to focus and do what I knew how to do.

We were once again broken up into small groups, where we learned two different combinations. Her group went first, and she did well. Despite my earlier pep talk, I had to take several breaths to calm myself down. I kept saying to myself, *Focus, Jennifer, you got this.* We were both there to audition, so obviously they saw something in me and my dancing even though I had a much shorter professional history.

My group was called, and I remember walking out onto the floor, preparing to perform the routine, when I caught her looking at me. She wasn't looking at me in a mean way but in a competitive way. Like, *Show me whatcha got.*

When it was all said and done, I left there thinking that no matter what happened, I had danced my heart out. A few days later, I was at home, having just walked in from taking Peff's class, when a call came through around three thirty in the afternoon. I usually let the answering machine pick up, but for some reason, I decided to answer it.

"Hi, Jennifer, this is Violet Holmes. We'd like to offer you the Super Bowl halftime show with the Rockettes." I was stunned into complete silence. "Hello? Are you there?"

"Yes, yes," I finally stammered out. "Um, can I think about it?"

She seemed surprised by my question but agreed to give me some time. Of course I'd take the job. But I was so nervous, I couldn't figure out what to say when I had her on the phone. I'd never been good with on-the-spot questions. I was the type who needed time to digest the question and answer at my own pace.

This was a huge opportunity: my first professional dance job and a chance to perform in one of the largest nationally syndicated shows of all time. The Super Bowl XXII halftime show. I couldn't believe I'd gotten the job. I was officially a Rockette.

In order to gather my thoughts, I took a walk around my neighborhood, mind racing the entire time. Was I good enough to be a

Rockette? I imagined so since they offered me a position. This dream of mine was finally coming to fruition.

Returning half an hour later, I called Violet and accepted my place on the line for the halftime show. She was pleased by my acceptance and gave me the background information I needed to get started, including rehearsal dates, times, location, and what I needed to bring. As soon as I hung up with her, I got in touch with my mom and told her the great news. She was so happy for me. We laughed and talked for a while, just reminiscing about the hard work it took to get me to this place. She was so proud that I stayed the course and that my efforts had paid off. Not only would I be dancing professionally but I'd be on TV.

A few days passed and I was watching the 11:00 p.m. *Channel 4 News* with Sue Simmons. Sue Simmons said, "Radio City has just hired their first African American dancer." I was thinking, *Huh, that's great. I wonder who it is.* And then my mother called, and she was like, "Are you watching the news? Oh my God, Jennifer, is that you?" I honestly wasn't sure. So I said, "I don't know, Mom," and she was like, "Well, who else could it be?"

When we hung up, I got to thinking. *Wow, maybe it is me.* Nobody had said anything about breaking any kind of color barriers, so I didn't want to assume.

Once I began my new position, Radio City told me that I was indeed the first Black woman to dance on the line. They told me there would be interviews, so I would be put in media training for preparation. The appearances included *Good Morning America* and *The Today Show*, as well as engaging with newspaper and magazine reporters.

I was through the moon that I had finally landed not only an incredible job but one with the famed Rockettes, so I was happy to do as they'd asked. I was called in to have a private meeting with Violet by the PR person. Violet was sitting behind her desk in her usual sweatshirt and high-water pants. As a dancer, I understood the comfort of rehearsal clothes, so I didn't think twice. During the meeting, I was briefed on a *New York Times* article where I was told Violet had been misquoted. Although they didn't go into detail about what the comment actually was, the woman from PR explained that Violet was misunderstood and to not address anyone about it. Violet was silent for the majority of the meeting, yet at the end, she shook her finger at me and said, "I'm not teaching you any choreography early," then folded her hands on her desk as if to dismiss me. I was taken aback because I had not asked to be taught anything without the group, so I wasn't sure where that response had originated. I often wondered if she was joking or implying that I wasn't good enough.

I guess I'll never know.

At the time of the article, in 1982, the NAACP was very active and aware of the lack of diversity on the line. They put pressure on Radio City to hire more women of color. Hazel N. Dukes, the New York State NAACP president, was quoted as saying, "They stayed lily-white all these years. . . . When I hear 'White Christmas,' to me it doesn't mean Caucasian Christmas; it means American Christmas."

I didn't allow the negative opinions of people like Violet to discourage me. Their attitudes only motivated me and made me want to push harder to prove my worth. This is one of the difficulties of being "a first." You are held to an almost impossible standard and have to work harder just to prove yourself. I was also dealing with a bit of self-doubt, and what's worse is that I didn't feel I could confide in anyone who could understand the pressures I was going through. It was pure determination and my love of dance that got me through. I wanted to be onstage, wanted to wear those lavish costumes, rhinestones, lashes, and red lipstick, then after my performance walk out of that backstage door. I would not give up so easily.

When I appeared on the front page of the *Post*, I was in a whirlwind and still working my telemarketing job. I knew I was going to quit at some point, but I wasn't sure of the process. I had never quit a job before and wasn't sure how to go about it. I went to work that day as I normally did, and upon completing my shift, I told my managers I wouldn't be coming back. They looked at me, lifted the newspaper, and gave me a huge smile. "We know" was all they said. They hadn't even expected me to come into work.

During that period, I was bounced from one interview to the next, along with a slew of photoshoots. I was so overwhelmed that I couldn't even think straight. *How should I do my hair? Is this makeup too much? Do my clothes look okay?* It was all a blur. I remember seeing everything happening around me, but I couldn't fully grasp it.

///////

Before the first day of rehearsals, I was assured by PR that there would be no media present. This would allow me to get comfortable within the line, adjust to the choreography, and meet some of the ladies without any added pressure. I was learning two dance combinations and Rockette technique and language. The interviews, the intensity of the performance, my nerves, and adrenaline combined to create a demanding situation to manage. Nevertheless, I cherished every second. I was engaging in what I adored. It wasn't Broadway, but it was akin to achieving stardom.

We did the lineup first, which means standing shoulder to shoulder, and I was positioned next to Barbara. Next we broke into two lines, front and back. I was in the front but wanted desperately to be in the back so I could follow the girl in front if needed. This was all new to me, and I didn't want to stick out if I made a mistake. I was focused on trying to keep up, since new choreography always took a couple days to sink in. Upon learning the first few counts of eight, I was told to go and get fitted for our costumes. The Rockettes had an in-house seamstress, so costumes were made at the Music Hall. They measured just about every part of my body, my head, neck, arms, bust, wrists, waist, legs, you name it. It was imperative that the costume fit perfectly to the dancer's body. When you are well put together, you may find yourself exuding a more confident demeanor, dancing with a sense of purpose, and effortlessly engaging with the audience.

My breath caught in my throat as I tried on the bodysuit that would accentuate my long leg line. My jacket with tails (I had never worn tails before) and my top hat fit perfectly. The second costume consisted of short shorts, another amazing leg line, a pink football jersey, and a football helmet. It was the very first time I experienced the sheer delight of a garment embracing me in all the right places, evoking a comfort and confidence that I had never felt before. As I caught my reflection in the mirror, I knew instantly that I was in the big leagues, where every stitch and seam was tailored to perfection. And I loved it. The entire process took about an hour, and then I was sent back up to the rehearsal hall. I could hear the music as I approached and could tell they had progressed a great deal since I'd left. I got a bit nervous as I stepped inside the rehearsal hall. They had added traveling time steps, changing lines, cramp roll turns, and were in perfect precision. I knew I'd be up all night in my kitchen practicing. Worse, I looked at my spot and saw a news crew standing in front of it.

Violet's eyes immediately landed on me, and she called out for the ladies to take it from the top. I took my place and gave the crew a tight smile. The pianist started playing the piano, and the cameraman got down on one knee so he could film my feet. I began dancing steps I barely knew, and soon things went from bad to total crash-and-burn disaster. I didn't know what I was doing and was all over the place.

"Hold it, ladies," Violet said, looking at me. She clapped her hands, and the music stopped. Walking directly in front of me— and the news crew—she told the pianist to take it half-time, then danced right there with my front to her back as I followed along. It seemed to me as if her actions were intentionally choreographed, conveying a subtle message that insinuated, *See, we tried to hire a Black girl. And clearly she doesn't know what she's doing. Now you have it on tape.*

Was this something she wanted on the news? Showing everyone how the Black one needed extra help? Who knows, but I could tell the reporter and cameraman felt bad for me, though there was nothing anyone could do.

I felt defeated. To be honest, I didn't know what kind of footage the camera crew got, if anything. I only knew I had to do better. It took a few days, but I finally learned the combinations and Rockette technique, like guiding to stay in line, toeing the line, heeling the line, and on the line, to keep formation. The rest of rehearsal was spent making sure to perfect those steps. From morning till night, my schedule was packed with rehearsals, interviews, and photoshoots. I would go home and review the routines I had learned that day and practice well into the wee hours of the morning. We practiced six days a week, seven hours a day, for weeks. There was no downtime to process or absorb the enormity of what was happening—how my life was changing, my new role, and the impact on other Black women auditioning to become Rockettes. I was taking it one day at a time, focusing on learning the show to deliver a flawless Super Bowl performance. Several weeks later, it was time to head to San Diego.

When we got on the plane, the flight crew announced over the loudspeaker that the Rockettes were on board, and we received a round of applause. I felt warm inside. During the flight, I remember seeing some of the ladies standing in the back of the plane, having a smoke, chatting with a few passengers. Smoking was allowed at that time, so this was pretty normal. About halfway through the flight, Brian, who was the assistant to the woman who ran PR, was sent to let me know his boss wanted to speak to me as soon as we got to the hotel. I thought maybe there were some interviews lined up in California, so I thought nothing of it.

Maria Hill, my friend from rehearsal, joined me as we gathered our things to deplane. We decided to room together since we had become fast friends. I was starving, and there were a couple ladies going to get a bite to eat and see what the city had to offer. I was happy to join them but remembered I was supposed to meet with PR. I waited for a while in the lobby of the hotel, but when I didn't see Brian, I figured I'd catch up with PR later on.

We went to TGI Fridays and washed down our meals with soft drinks after our attempt to get wine coolers was dissuaded. We got carded when we tried to order them, and none of us were old enough to drink. By the time we reached the hotel, Brian was pacing back and forth in the lobby. He nervously reiterated that the head of PR wanted to see me. His actions caused anxiety to build within me, and I wondered what it was she wanted to speak to me about.

The woman running PR told me to sit down when I arrived at her suite, while she paced the room, smoking cigarettes. As soon as I sat down, she looked me square in the eyes and said, "Nobody cares about you. Nobody cares about your story. Nobody cares about you being the first Black woman to dance on the line. Nobody cares. You're old news. You should consider yourself lucky to even be here." She took a long drag of her cigarette, as if a huge weight had been lifted from her shoulders, then stared at me like she'd made some profound speech. I'm guessing she was boiling hot over 1) my being Black and her clearly thinking I didn't deserve to be there, and 2) the fact that I went to have lunch with my newfound friends and made her wait.

I was speechless.

Had she really called me down there to "put me in my place"?

Glancing at Brian, I could tell he was mortified. I just got up and left. When I returned to my room, Maria and our dance mate Veronica wanted to know what PR had said. I was so embarrassed, I told them it was nothing.

That night I went back out with Maria and Veronica, plus a few other women from the line, and we enjoyed ourselves. However, for years after that, I thought that I was fortunate to be in the position rather than feeling that I had earned my place. The PR woman's words knocked the wind out of my sails. I figured no one cared about me or this breakthrough for the African American community.

Even though I was on the most amazing journey of my career, I felt insignificant. But I kept my feelings inside and smiled through it. It didn't matter what they thought. I was there and would be performing with Chubby Checker for the NFL halftime show.

7

The Best Is Yet to Come

Returning home from San Diego, I was still on cloud nine. Knowing my family had been there to support me while having the opportunity to tour a new city was one of the best experiences of my life. But now reality sank in. I had not been hired on to become a part of the *Christmas Spectacular* and honestly had no idea how the Rockette organization operated full-time outside of the financial aspect. Sure, I'd been paid handsomely for my participation in the show, but I needed something stable. Something long-term. By this time, I had moved out of New York and had spent several months continuing my dance classes, auditioning, and trying to figure out what came next for me.

I had just turned twenty-one, so my good friend Erica and I would hang out at local bars and restaurants to wind down. One evening we headed to TGI Fridays in Parsippany and shared good conversation, laughs, and a few drinks, just having a nice time. Suddenly, we noticed two guys sitting across from us, enjoying drinks as well. We didn't pay them much attention, but one of them kept staring at me. Erica was like, "Hey, that guy keeps looking at you, you know." But I continued enjoying her company and conversation and ignored my admirer. A little while later, the guy and his friend came over to us, and they introduced themselves as Matt and David. Matt immediately got my attention and started flirting with me.

Erica and I had seen them speaking with some young ladies beforehand, so Erica, as bold as she is, asked, "Um, aren't you with those girls over there?" Matt looked toward the women as if he had no idea who she was speaking about. "Yeah," he said, "we were only hanging out with them. We'd rather be over here, talking to you guys." Erica and I shared a laugh and invited them to sit with us. We ordered more drinks and a little food and chatted the night away. As the evening wound down, Matt asked for my phone number. I took a moment to think about it but had to admit I wasn't quite ready to date. I was focused on finding myself. I didn't need any distractions. Matt was surprisingly sweet about it and reassured me that it was no problem; he was just happy to make my acquaintance. He and David left, and Erica and I stayed for a short while longer before calling it a night ourselves.

The following weekend, while hanging out at Bennigan's in Morristown—which is in the opposite direction of Parsippany—Erica and I saw Matt and David. I couldn't believe it. I'd run into him two weekends in a row. He was at the bar with David, and just like last time, he caught our attention before coming over to our table. We had a great time conversing and getting to know one another, and again he asked me for my number. I politely declined, as I had done previously, stating the same reasoning I'd given him before. He looked disappointed, but, the gentleman that he was, he didn't press and wished us both a good night.

The next week, while at a bar called the Fireside in Denville, we saw Matt and David once more. At this point, I was thinking, *Oh my God, are they following us?* The odds of seeing him three weekends in a row at different places was a strange coincidence. I was starting to think it was kismet that we kept running into each other. As always, we had a nice night of conversation, drinks, and food.

Not long after our latest encounter, the County College of Morris asked me to do a campaign for the school. They had just started a billboard campaign where they'd advertise successful students who had graduated from there. Though I had left, they still wanted me to participate—and be one of the first at that. I was happy to do it, so we set up a time for the photoshoot. The billboard read *I started right at CCM*, and then it included my picture, name, and had *Radio City, Rockette*, below it. This was exciting and a positive omen of things to come. A sign that I was meant to be there, though I'd begun auditioning for other gigs.

In September 1988, Violet called and asked if I wanted to join the *Christmas Spectacular*. This time I didn't need to call her back. It was an immediate yes. Rehearsals started in October, and the show was set to open in November. I couldn't wait to get started.

The Christmas show was a totally different experience than the Super Bowl. The rehearsals were more demanding, and I had to learn a repertoire of dances that the seasoned ladies already knew. The production ran ninety minutes long; I'd never performed for that length of time before, so I had to build some serious stamina to keep my strength up for practice and ultimately the performance.

In order to prepare, we practiced all eight numbers, day in and day out, perfecting each move until we were completely in unison. Precision and elegance was—and still is—the Rockette technique.

My first rehearsal started promptly at 10:00 a.m. Most of the girls had already been there for at least an hour, chatting, warming up, and fixing their dressing tables, waiting to be weighed in. Since they were mostly seasoned Rockettes, many of them had their own personal dressing tables. I, of course, did not. Searching the room, I had a tough time finding a spot for myself. Finally, one of the women offered me a seat at the table next to her. She was originally from Queens and had beautiful long hair and a thick New York accent.

Some of the girls advised me on the kinds of foods to eat and snacks to bring to keep my energy up. Water was super important, so I made sure to bring it to every rehearsal in order to stay hydrated. Maintaining healthy habits assisted with weigh-ins, another important factor of being a Rockette, which happened right before rehearsals started. We were given separate weight ranges depending on our body fat test, and my weight range was between 120 and 126. If you fell three pounds below or three pounds above, you were still okay; they at least gave you that leeway. This was my saving grace between water weight and slight weight gain during my period. But if you were over or under by four pounds or more, you would have two weeks to either lose or gain the weight, and then they would reweigh you. If you were still not within your range, you were taken out of the production for that year.

Across the room was a dressing table, and it was filled with food. Bagels, muffins, fruit, pastries, scrambled eggs—you name it, it was there. There was a woman sitting at the table, but she wouldn't eat. I couldn't understand why until I overheard the girls saying, "Let Shannon get weighed in first so she can eat."

The weigh-in room was located on the fifth floor, just inside Violet's office. There were women standing in line, some in their bras and panties, others in robes with nothing on underneath or in leotards. I stood there, heart pounding, waiting to get weighed in. When it was my turn to go, Violet and her assistant, Joyce, were inside the room. I stepped on the scale in my leotard and tights, holding my breath as they slid the bars back and forth, measuring my weight. I weighed in at 123 pounds and released the breath I'd been holding. Violet said, "I'll see you upstairs," as Joyce wrote my weight down in a ledger. I retreated to the dressing room, where the ladies were finally eating, sipping coffee, or having a smoke in the stairwell. I had a bite to eat, then grabbed my tap and kick shoes and joined everyone as we made our way upstairs to the spacious rehearsal hall. I vividly recall riding up in the same elevator I had taken to the audition. With a mix of nerves and anticipation, I hoped to keep pace with the proceedings. The presence of Maria, my friend and Super Bowl roommate, provided a comforting sense of familiarity.

There in that rehearsal studio, I discovered my passion all over again. The mirrors, the floor, the photographs on the wall of Rockettes through the years in different costumes, the kick line tape, and even Ethel at the piano—they rekindled my love for the art.

The first part of rehearsal was getting into your lineup for the famous kick line. The optical illusion. They were placing us in and out of the line, trying to get the girls in size order by shoulders. This was important since this was where we'd be throughout the production and how we were tracked for formations. Then we began training for the soldier fall. This was one of the hardest and most intricate techniques to learn, and girls could get injured if not done correctly. You could blow out your knee, sprain your ankle, or attain any number of ailments that could have you out for the season.

We'd break the line into sections before the entire line performed the move. A dancer would support the back of the girl in front of her by sliding her arms underneath the girl's in a straight line, and then slowly fall backward, stiff as a board, one by one, into each other. It took a ton of core and arm strength—not to mention trust in your fellow Rockettes, as they had to be able to support your weight as you fell backward into each other's arms. This was particularly true for the very last girl, who was essentially holding the weight of most of the group. Once you mastered that, it was only up from there.

Each day we learned the routines for "Christmas in New York," "Rag Dolls," "Carol of the Bells" and the "Reindeer" number, along with the famous chorus line of kicking legs at the show's end. Most times I'd learn the numbers, then go home and practice for hours and hours until my feet hurt, head spun, and I passed out from sheer exhaustion, only to wake up and do it all over again the next day. I loved feeling special whenever I walked in and out of the golden Radio City stage doors. It was magical each and every time.

Rehearsals could get overwhelming with media interviews, costume fittings, catching up on choreography, etc. I would find myself missing steps and ending up in my own line, breaking formation. The choreography was quite complex. Once I walked out of rehearsal because I was so overwhelmed, I started to cry. Violet came and got me, and the other women were patient with me, telling me the rules of the kick line, more than willing to help me correct my steps. A lot of the girls knew how to guide perfectly, going from one line to three seamlessly.

There was another situation, when Violet stopped rehearsal and looked over at me just before a Rockette called me out. "Look at her, she's in her own line." I felt so embarrassed that I never stepped out of line again. Instead of giving up, I kept at it and worked harder to perfect my steps. I vividly recall the time when, while rehearsing "Christmas in New York" with different line changes and formations, Violet gave me a subtle nod and smile during our run-through. It may have gone unnoticed by others, but to me, it was a significant affirmation that I was heading in the right direction. That nod and smile meant the world to me.

Opening night, my very first at Radio City Music Hall, was incredible. Everything was abuzz. The ushers, the audience, the orchestra. I felt more alive than I'd ever felt in my entire life. The ladies were laughing and putting on lashes, stretching, practicing, and getting prepared for our performance. There were two dressing rooms on the third floor, one called the Big Rox; the other, the Little Rox. The Big Rox was the dressing room that could house most of the thirty-eight dancers—about twenty-five. The Little Rox had less of a crowd and was quieter and more mellow.

I got a call from security on the house phone, saying I had received a delivery. When I got there, I had a beautiful bouquet of long-stemmed roses. I brought them to my dressing room and discovered a card that read, "Wishing you a fantastic Opening Night.

Matt." I smiled immediately. When we crossed paths, I never revealed that I was a Rockette. He must have seen the billboard. What a heady feeling that was, that he'd seen me on a billboard.

I ran to the nearest pay phone and called him using the number he'd left on the card. I thanked him for the gorgeous bouquet and finally gave him my number, agreeing to go out on a date with him once the show concluded in January.

Everything after that moment was an absolute dream come true. I'll never forget the crowd, the curtain rising, and waiting in the wings for my debut performance in the legendary "The Wooden Soldiers." I was filled with excitement to then recount the first-ever kick line in "Christmas in New York" onstage, leading up to the powerful moment of the Nativity blessings and the captivating procession featuring camels and sheep.

In many ways, this experience marked a series of firsts for me. I had to adapt to rapid changes, particularly when it came to switching outfits multiple times throughout the performance. Mastering the choreography also meant becoming familiar with the offstage locations for changing. Each of us had her own designated space, and specific dressers were assigned to assist with costume changes. These dressers played a vital role in the show, preparing our outfits before the show began and tending to any wear and tear during the performance.

Our quick changes took place in small, cramped, offstage rooms. My quick change from "The Wooden Soldiers" to "Christmas in New York" occurred stage left, and I shared the space with a woman named Lucille. It became apparent that she harbored reservations about new additions to the troupe and did not welcome me, especially as a newcomer, maybe even as a Black woman. In the confined quarters of the quick-change room stage left, which housed eighteen ladies, Lucille accused me of encroaching on her space. As the season progressed, I made a deliberate effort to stay within my designated area, ensuring that my movements were contained within my allocated space. No matter my efforts or the presence of other women in the area, she seemed to single me out every time. She'd make public remarks about my presence in "her spot." Her comments grew increasingly louder with each instance, drawing the attention of everyone in the room. She would look up to the sky as if seeking divine intervention, roll her eyes, and audibly sigh. The dressers quickly noticed her antics and assured me that they would expedite my costume changes.

During subsequent shows, as the changes approached, I focused on swift and efficient transitions. Lucille once again gazed upward to the sky, but this time she proceeded to strike my foot and shin, berating me for invading her space. Each word was accentuated by a swift hit to my leg. Reflecting on this, I realize I should have stood up for myself, but I was so shaken by her persistence and physical aggression, I couldn't react. Mary Beth, a true Southern belle, intervened by raising her voice and instructing Lucille to stop. She then confronted Lucille about her actions and encouraged me to never tolerate such behavior from anyone ever again.

Setsuko Maruhashi was the first Asian woman on the line, in 1985, and we'd often do media appearances together. During a rehearsal, Sets approached me and remarked, "I am the first Asian Rockette, and you are the first African American Rockette," before walking away. This encounter left a lasting impression on me, as it highlighted the significant impact we, as minorities, had on the Rockette line. The unspoken truth was that we were ushering in a new era. She wanted me to be aware of the ground we were breaking and that sometimes it came with certain challenges. Perhaps Violet accurately pinpointed the issue when she made those remarks about women of color being seen as a distraction, even though the organization chose never to talk about it. For a significant period of time, I could envision their audience consisting mainly of fair-haired, blue-eyed children. However, now they had families from diverse racial backgrounds attending the theater.

The best part was that I had my own family there to show their support. My grandparents would often come into New York to see the show. I was a local celebrity to my loved ones, and the support I received from the Black community was beyond anything I could have imagined. The PR I'd been doing had shone a light on my acceptance into the Rockettes, and that was no small feat. Families would send letters, and for every piece of hate mail I received, I would get two more notes of admiration, pushing me to keep going and keep making the Black community proud. To have little Black girls tell me how much they loved dance and how much I inspired them to want to pursue dance . . . it took me back to that moment in the Majestic Theatre, when I said that very same thing watching Stephanie Mills perform.

Within a few years, we were doing at least four, sometimes five or six shows a day. I'd break my day down by resting in between shows to rejuvenate myself for the next performance. Meaning I'd do one show, then sleep during my first break. At the conclusion of the second show, I might get a snack and some water. Then on the third, I'd shower and maybe snack and hydrate again. Following the last show, I'd go home, rest, then come back the next day to start the process over again.

On this day in particular, I was on my third break. I decided to go to the large rehearsal hall to do some stretching exercises before taking a shower. I liked being in the big hall because I normally had it to myself. It was a great way to unwind and clear my mind after a long day. Once I completed my stretch routine, I came back down to the dressing room to get ready to shower. When I got there, I saw one of the women on the line sitting at her vanity. She was half dressed in her T-shirt and tights. As I turned the corner, I looked at her, and she was staring at herself in the mirror, eyes sunken. She had painted her face with the darkest foundation she could find. It was so dark that it startled me upon first glance. She looked at me with a deadpan expression, almost smirking at her reflection. I could feel my blood bubbling over. This woman had the audacity to apply her makeup to imitate someone in blackface. A few girls gathered around her and thought this was the funniest thing ever. "Oh geez," they said. "You're hilarious." Others seemed just as surprised as I was but didn't say anything, only smiled. I ignored them and went to my spot, looked at myself in the mirror, and reminded myself of who I was, where I came from, and that no matter what they said or did, I was standing on the shoulders of my ancestors. I was not alone. I was just as good a dancer as they were, if not better, and I would not allow anyone to intimidate me. I took a deep breath, gathered myself, then undressed to take my shower and proceeded to have a great last show for that day.

Another instance comes to mind: when a simple wardrobe request escalated. As I readied myself for a performance, I cast a quick glance at my tights and silently wished they could match my skin tone. I then casually asked the dresser if it would be possible to obtain some darker tights. I was not anticipating an immediate response, perhaps thinking it could be accommodated the following day or later in the week. To my surprise, she met my inquiry with hostility. Perplexed, I attempted to explain the reason behind my request, emphasizing that I was not expecting an instant resolution, especially considering our upcoming performance. Instead of listening, she raised her voice, causing a scene. I spoke softly, trying to redirect the conversation, but she continued to yell. I stood there in disbelief as she exclaimed, "Who do you think you are? We're not making any changes for you. That's the costume. And if you don't like it, you can leave." I hurriedly finished dressing and made my way to the stage, where I could still hear her speaking about the costumes remaining unchanged. It was deeply embarrassing. I had no intention of leaving the stage and giving up my dream of dancing. I did not take it personally. I kept that same mentality when it came to people having a hard time accepting a Black woman on the line.

While all this was happening, I was still trying to navigate life in the big city. Times Square was filled with gangbangers, prostitutes, drug addicts, and all sorts of unsavory characters. And though I was more familiar with the subway, it was tough trying to get from point A to point B safely, particularly late at night.

Despite encountering obstacles, I drew strength and motivation from my family, Bible scriptures like "And this, too, shall pass," and the song "The Best Is Yet to Come." Those lyrics constantly reminded me to maintain a positive and hopeful outlook, offering the encouragement I needed to persist. The song urged me to pursue my aspirations, and during challenging times, propelled me forward, undeterred by the opinions of others.

The best is yet to come.

CROWNING ACHIEVEMENT — Jennifer Jones of Randolph tap-danced her way to the Miss Morris County crown Saturday night. Story, Page A3.

Miss Morris County 1989

8

A Breath of Fresh Air

My relationship with Matt was somewhat of a whirlwind romance. Being with him felt like a fairy tale come true. He was kind, charming, and sweet, and he pushed me to be the best version of myself. He recognized my value and respected my determination to follow my dream to pursue dance. He believed that I was a good, hardworking person, and there were often moments when I sensed that he had more faith in me than I had in myself.

We went out all the time for lunch and dinner, and took road trips whenever our schedules allowed. We genuinely enjoyed spending time together, even if it was pizza and wine in the backyard or cuddling while watching movies on the couch. Matt was twenty-three years old, just two years older than me. His grandfather had come from Italy to the United States during the Great Depression to create a better life for his family. Matt's mother was a model from the Netherlands, so Matt was half-Italian, half-Dutch. His family owned a number of apartment buildings on the Upper East

Side in Manhattan, so he worked in the family business. He could make his own hours, allowing him a certain flexibility when it came to us making plans.

As soon as he and his brother were old enough, they moved into the family's summer lake house in New Jersey while their parents remained in New York. We'd often spend time at the lake house, especially when I was off. We were inseparable. I grew to love Matt just as much as he loved me.

However, that kind of love and intensity sometimes overwhelmed us. Nowadays some people might label it as toxic, but back then we were passionate, and our desires and emotions often got the best of us. We would frequently go through a cycle of breaking up and making up, as the old Stylistics song used to say. This pattern persisted throughout our relationship, but we always maintained love for each other and consistently found our way back.

In 1989, Matt issued a challenge for me to participate in the Miss Morris County competition. He playfully dared me over dinner one evening to enter the contest. Initially, I was unsure, but he persisted, discussing the prospect of using that as leverage to establish an aerobics studio down the line. He suggested my being the first Black Rockette and a Miss Morris County could help make the studio a more lucrative venture. Encouraged by this, I decided to enter the competition. If I won, I had the opportunity to progress to the Miss New Jersey competition. At the conclusion of the *Christmas Spectacular*, I found myself with ample time to dedicate to the pageant.

I was partnered with the previous year's winner, who showed me the ropes, walking me through every step of the event. It was even more competitive than I imagined. I never had my sights on being Miss America, but I did watch the pageant every year on TV. I knew the categories well—swimsuit, evening gown, talent—and I was thrilled to compete in each one. I learned how to stand, wave, walk; my partner put me in winning contention. She made sure no stone went unturned.

While going through the process, I could see some of the girls really rooting for one another. The shared tips and tricks and the comradery made me feel more at home. Even though this was a highly competitive event—some of the contestants had attended pageantry schools to train—many of the girls were humble and gracious. I enjoyed the experience and had fun shopping with my mom at specialty stores for my swimsuit, gowns, and other necessary garments for my segments.

Preparing for the event, I thought back to a time on the line when my fellow dancers weren't as nice or helpful. Whenever I napped during my breaks, I pushed a few chairs together so I could lie down. One evening I was lying down out of sight, and I could hear some of the ladies come into the area, chatting. They were speaking about how weird one of the girls was and how nobody really liked this girl. They went on to say she was antisocial and never joined in on the last-show dance parties, which we'd have at the end of the last show. I thought, *Wow, they really don't like this girl.* I wondered who they were talking about but kept my eyes closed and never moved or made a sound. One of the women came around the corner where I was tucked away and noticed me lying there on the chairs. I pretended to be asleep. Suddenly, I heard a loudly whispered "Oh my God, oh my God," followed by a little giggle. I was like, *Holy crap, they're talking about me*. It was clear by her reaction that she hadn't known I was there. They quickly left the room, laughing quietly, probably thinking I hadn't heard them. As with the previous incidents, I never said anything.

Thankfully, I didn't encounter anything like that while working on the pageant. As the competition grew near, I kept my eye on the first runner-up from the previous year. Being first runner-up is a hefty duty, and she obviously had the skill to come so close to winning. There were a great many benefits to partaking in the event, even if you didn't win. Pageants boosted one's self-confidence, strengthened one's skills in public speaking, and opened the door to making lifetime friends and connections.

The time had come, and the competition was in full swing. After the swimsuit and talent segments, the pageant would conclude with the evening gown round. Following the final contestant's graceful walk, all participants were summoned back to the stage, where we assembled in a semicircle in anticipation of the crowning. The host proceeded to call forth five girls who had placed, asking them to step aside to form a separate line. Among them, my name was called, along with the previous year's runner-up.

The announcement of the results commenced with the fourth runner-up, and given my prior achievement of securing fourth place in Little Miss Ebony, I presumed this would be my ranking. However, when a name was called that wasn't my own, followed by the announcement of the third-place winner, I found myself astonished. Second place was declared, also leaving me in awe. Subsequently, there were two of us standing side by side onstage, one of us poised to be crowned the winner.

Miss Morris County was revealed to be Jennifer Jones, and ecstatic cheers and applause could be heard from Matt, my mother, and my nana in the audience.

Succeeding my victorious walk, I dealt with a flurry of paperwork, autograph requests, and photography appointments for the local newspaper. As I basked in the afterglow of victory, still adorned in my elegant gown, Matt casually approached me and whispered, "See, I told you, you would win." I couldn't contain my beaming smile. It wasn't until the news was publicized in the newspaper that I discovered I was the first African American to claim the title. I was ecstatic to have attained this momentous achievement.

The Miss New Jersey competition was much more intense. There was an abundance of contestants, one from each county. I felt like a fish out of water. It seemed like most of the ladies knew one another, what to do, where to go, and the protocols to follow. They weren't as forthcoming as the competitors in Miss Morris County. During preliminary judging, I didn't place and was let go. I had no hard feelings and was grateful for the experience. Though the role I played in Morris County history opened doors for other women of color, I realized that pageantry competition was not where I belonged. I celebrated my win as Miss Morris County by attending local parades and events, as well as business grand openings. It was memorable, and I hope to have inspired others who competed afterward.

Matt and I had been together a little over a year, and he encouraged me to take my dreams a step further and partner with him on an aerobics studio. We had discussed the possibility before, but I had my reservations, since I'd never owned or managed a business before. Matt assured me that with both of us involved, we could be successful. He reminded me that my Rockette background coupled with the MMC win would be great for business. He would handle the business side, and I would take care of the instructor side of things. I started to feel more confident that we could make it work.

In 1990, we rented a space in a strip mall in Rockaway, New Jersey, and the Jennifer Jones Dance and Fitness Center was born. At that time, there was only one other aerobics studio in the area, called Unique Aerobics, so it was an obvious decision to proceed with our own studio. There were no big chains like LA Fitness or World Gym, so we did not have a ton of competition. As the first to offer step aerobics alongside regular aerobics, we were excited to introduce both workouts to attract members. This decision was based on our belief that step aerobics classes and other dynamic exercises would be ideal for capturing enthusiasm.

Our plan worked. Being the first studio to offer these classes made us a success. Our studio provided a range of offerings, including step aerobics, interval training classes, and a small room equipped with free weights, treadmills, bikes, and StairMasters. Furthermore, I initiated teaching dance classes to underprivileged children through Easterseals and UNICEF, as it brought me great joy to provide them with the opportunity to embrace dance despite their families' financial constraints. Although our studio was not large, it had a significant impact within the community.

Operating the Jennifer Jones Dance and Fitness Center brought with it a plethora of emotions: a blend of worry, fear, and excitement rolled into one. I remember the night before the grand opening, I confided in Matt, expressing my doubts about my ability to take on the role of boss, overseeing twelve aerobics instructors and managing customer service. He reminded me that this endeavor was a joint effort; he would be with me every step of the way, and it would be beneficial for both of us. With a successful studio, I felt a sense of relief wash over me. My thoughts and insecurities were what had fueled my fear. Post-opening, I found joy in engaging with members, teaching classes, and managing the day-to-day operations. We celebrated this milestone by indulging in pizza from our favorite pizzeria and savoring a bottle of wine. Cheers!

My mom and I had grown closer. She still lived in Randolph with my sister Peaches, and Cheryl had relocated to New York. I didn't have much contact with my dad, but my grandparents and the rest of my family were present. We got together for holidays and other special occasions when my Radio City schedule allowed. We spoke regularly, and they continued to come to many of my performances. I also kept in touch with a few of my friends from high school who remained in the area. One of my instructors was vegan and had educated me on how to transition to a plant-based lifestyle. These dietary changes had me looking and feeling amazing.

Throughout the holiday season, I would stay in one of Matt's apartments in Manhattan so I could be closer to Radio City. I now had a condo in New Jersey on Oak Street in Rockaway, so even though I spent a lot of time with Matt, we weren't living together. My condo was right down the street from the fitness center, making it easy to get to and from work. Though we had decided to open the business together, Matt thought it would be a good idea to keep our relationship private. His reasoning was that if members knew we were together, it wouldn't be good for business. He was the business mind, so I took his advice.

At the time, Rockettes made approximately $1,200 per week during the Christmas season. And if there was a tree lighting, Macy's Thanksgiving Day Parade, or any other publicity, we'd get additional pay. Holiday pay was also given if we worked Veterans Day, Thanksgiving, Christmas, or New Year's. Overtime pay was also available if dancers performed more than three shows in one day. All in all, I made upwards of $40,000 a year, far more than I'd ever made at any job. Add this to what was being made by the studio, and I was living quite comfortably.

I hired about twelve instructors when we opened, and we eventually hired a manager so I wouldn't have to be at the studio 24/7. This gave me the opportunity to revel in the joyful Christmas season in New York City. I loved the flexibility of it all. One week, I'd be leisurely strolling to and from the theater, breathing in the crisp, fresh air and admiring the people entering and exiting the buildings. Venturing down Fifth Avenue, I'd marvel at the delightful sight of festive tree-adorned shops and Christmas-decorated buildings or make the occasional stroll past FAO Schwarz, often considered the embodiment of the Christmas spirit. And then another week, I'd be driving along the suburban streets of New Jersey and into the parking lot of my business. It made me appreciate the stark contrast between my life as a dancer and that of an entrepreneur. The best of both worlds.

It was a great distraction from the events happening in Matt's and my relationship that I didn't want to face.

///////

Radio City announced that the Rockettes would be going on tour in *The Great Radio City Spectacular* starring Susan Anton. Following three years of co-ownership of the studio and several disputes with Matt, I made the decision to leave it all behind. I wanted to see what the world had in store for me. We sold the business to one of our instructors, and I set off to explore the country.

I had a great opportunity to work with Maurice Hines and Joe Layton for a once-in-a-lifetime experience. The tour began in Buffalo, New York, and traveled to places like Rochester, New York; Peoria, Illinois; Tempe and Tucson, Arizona; Sacramento, California; and Detroit, Michigan. There were twenty-eight Rockettes who traveled. Four of the twenty-eight were called "swings," who were basically our backups if anyone got sick or injured.

One of my best memories was visiting Seattle and going to the Space Needle. It was exactly what I needed: a break from business and everything else I had going on. The tour would stay for a week in each city, sometimes allowing us a brief moment to sightsee and be tourists. Most times, the week passed us by in a blur, and it was hard to keep track of where we were. The cast, crew, and musicians became a traveling family.

I had to admit, although I didn't leave on the best of terms, I missed Matt. I also missed my family and was starting to feel homesick. I kept telling myself to enjoy it, that this was a character-building adventure, but I couldn't deny the feelings that crept up inside me each day the tour progressed. It took me back to a memory I had as a child. My mom had signed Cheryl and me up for sleepaway camp. It was only for two weeks and wasn't too far from home. The schedule was chock-full of fun activities and daily events. Once we were registered with the camp counselor, my mom told us to have fun and went on her way. Although everyone appeared to be having a good time, including my sister, who blended right in with the other kids, I just couldn't get comfortable. I didn't like to be away from home and wasn't the best at mingling with my peers.

I went into the counselor's office, where about five counselors were milling about. I told them I didn't feel good. They were pretty young, mostly teenagers with an easy-breezy summer job. They tried to ease my fears and told me I would be fine, that it would take a minute to adjust, and once I did, I'd have a great time. When I repeated that I didn't feel well, they offered me the phone to call my mom.

Dialing the number, I quickly placed the receiver to my ear, waiting for her to pick up. Upon hearing her voice, I explained that I felt ill and needed her to come and get me. As she tried to convince me to stay, I threw up all over the place. The counselors jumped back and pushed their chairs out of the way. The phone, desk, and chair were soiled with vomit. The counselor closest to me told my mom she'd have to come get me, and then they sent me to the nurse's office to wait to be picked up.

Though this tour was nowhere near as bad as that summer camp experience, I did miss the comfort of home. No longer a child, I focused on performing and enjoying different parts of the country. Our next destination was Tempe, Arizona, and I took full advantage of our time there. A bunch of us went horseback riding although it was Christmastime. The skies were clear, and the weather was perfect, so we took advantage of the many outdoor activities we couldn't do while on the East Coast. The guide took us on gorgeous trails with a variety of cacti, then made us an open-pit breakfast before we took the horses back. When I returned to the hotel, I checked in at the desk to retrieve any messages I might have gotten. The receptionist said, "Oh, these are for you," and collected flowers upon flowers, six dozen in total. Matt had surprised me. There were so many flowers, they had to use a cart to bring them up. Things were definitely looking brighter.

///////

Matt asked if he could visit me in Arizona. I agreed. When I arrived at the hotel, I was surprised to see him in the lobby. The moment was bittersweet. Seeing his familiar face jarred so many memories and history. He felt like home.

We talked after my performance that night, and he told me how much he missed me. He expressed that, rather than my having these experiences alone, we should be making memories together. He painted a beautiful picture of a full life for us. One way to get us back on track, he proposed, was to take full advantage of the mountains that we were encapsulated in. A hot-air balloon ride would be a wonderful memory we could share.

We reached the open field and were introduced to an engineer who helped us pick out our balloon. Once we chose which balloon we wanted to go in, we were given instructions, and then they assisted us as we blew up our own balloon. We got inside the small basket, and I was a ball of nerves, but Matt was fearless. He held my hand as the engineer fired up the balloon, and soon, we were being lifted off the ground. The view of the terrain was absolutely breathtaking. I had always vacationed on beaches and never realized the beauty of the mountains. Feeling the wind in my hair, the morning sun on my skin, and Matt by my side taking it all in was unforgettable. It was so serene, quiet, colorful, and majestic.

There was a truck that followed us below to make sure everything went okay. When it came time to land, I was petrified. The engineer told us we would be making a crash landing. As we got closer to our destination, the engineer said, "You should probably get down," and I dropped down so fast, I felt like I had become a part of the floor. Matt, however, wanted to see the whole thing and continued standing as we descended. Despite the rough landing, we managed to get down safely, and I had to rush out to rehearsal after. I snuck in without anyone noticing and had our incredible day on my mind the entire time.

Matt came to another tour stop in Maryland. After the show, we went out to a restaurant for a drink. As we drank and talked, he brought up how much he loved me and wanted to build a life with me. He spoke about a long-term commitment, a beautiful home, kids, and even a dog. This was music to my ears. I truly loved this man—we loved each other. And now here he was, making a grand gesture and telling me how magical we could be together.

As if right on cue, Elton John's "Circle of Life" came on, and it seemed like a sign since we were speaking about what our future together would look like. Suddenly, Matt got down on one knee and popped the question. "Jennifer, will you marry me?" I was staring at him like, *Is this a dream? Is he serious?* But as he gazed into my eyes, I knew this was real—*we* were real, and I could feel it, too. I told him, "Yes, I will marry you," and he stood up and gave me a long hug and a kiss.

I was the happiest woman in the world. Everything felt so right.

After I returned home from the tour, we set a date and celebrated our marriage a year later on June 17, 1995. The wedding ceremony was incredibly beautiful, and I was escorted down the aisle by my mother. My father attended but had been working a lot, so he wasn't available for rehearsals. The rest of my family was there as well. Our event planner meticulously arranged the decor at Matt's lakeside summer home, creating a breathtaking altar where we exchanged our vows. The reception area was adorned with elegant place settings, exquisite floral arrangements, and a live cellist serenading our arriving guests. Luminaries were strategically placed around the water, creating a mesmerizing spectacle at night while the water sprinklers produced a captivating fountain effect. Valet parking was organized to accommodate the limited parking in our driveway, ensuring that guests' cars wouldn't obstruct the neighbors. For the wedding ceremony, we enjoyed the performance of a three-piece orchestra, followed by a DJ and my cousin's band for the reception. Catering stations offered a wide array of food, including margaritas from our favorite Mexican restaurant, a pasta station, a meat-carving station, and a selection of fruits and cheeses. Matt and I selected a delightful tiramisu wedding cake from a charming local Italian restaurant. It was the storybook wedding I had always envisioned, and we had a splendid time with our family and friends.

Afterward we eagerly anticipated our two-week honeymoon in Italy. It felt as if everything I had ever yearned for in life and love was finally coming together harmoniously. I had a flourishing career in dance, a devoted husband, and my family close by. What could possibly go wrong?

9

Everything That Glitters
Ain't Gold

Our first year as newlyweds was absolute bliss. I experienced even more of what I knew to be true—that Matt was an incredible husband. We took care of each other, and life was running smoothly. I was still working as a Rockette, and he was still working in the family business.

Our two-week honeymoon in Italy was fabulous. It was fascinating to learn about Matt's Italian roots. By chance, we met some of his extended family. We had been walking around his grandfather's village of Puglia and asked if anyone knew his last name. We were shocked by the response. Everyone knew who his grandfather was, and soon we were sharing a drink with his distant relatives. Though we couldn't really engage in much conversation due to our limited knowledge of Italian, it was fun to be in one another's company. There was a lot of love and history there, and I was thankful to have had the opportunity to experience that together.

We toured Puglia, Rome, Venice, and Capri, shopped at the best stores, and tried as many restaurants as possible. Puglia had the most incredible olive platters, served with fresh-made bread that we could dip in olive oil. Then there was the hotel restaurant draped in olive vines that featured live music with a solo guitarist playing a song about *la luna*, the moon. Matt stood up and held out his hand, and I smiled, quickly placing my hand in his, as he pulled me in close for a dance. There was no dance floor, so we swayed to the music near our table, lost in each other's eyes. Even though the restaurant was full, it felt as if we were the only two people in the room. When the song ended, the other patrons, who had been watching, gave us a round of applause.

Rome had an ever-so-memorable pasta dish. Homemade pasta with "real" Italian tomato sauce, chunks of mozzarella, olives, and capers. In Venice, we walked around sightseeing at the river walk and museums while tasting the most delicious gelato. Capri served some of the most unforgettable Mediterranean dishes I've ever tasted. I literally ate my way through Italy and returned twenty pounds heavier. But I didn't care. We had the time of our lives. Our only focus was becoming comfortable with each other and getting adjusted to married life.

Now that I was home, I had just a few months to get myself back into shape. Rehearsals started in October, so I quickly fell into my usual routine. I joined a fitness center close to home and sometimes went for a walk or run around the lake before heading to the gym. Since we spent some overnights at Matt's parents' house in Pennsylvania, I would take long walks or jog during our visits.

I was able to get my weight down right on time and was thrilled to be back on Radio City's landmark stage once again. And we performed everywhere. The Christmas season wasn't just about the *Spectacular* but also entailed events at *The Today Show*, the Rockefeller Center Christmas Tree Lighting, and other opportunities around the city. I loved meeting people. Having the chance to interact with children and families was the icing on the cake. I was glad to be back to work.

As the show's season came to a close, I discovered my period was late. I attributed it to the intense exercise regimen since my return to the show. To be safe, I scheduled a doctor's appointment for after the show concluded. At my appointment, I found out I was pregnant. I was overjoyed. I went home feeling great and thought about the changes that would soon be happening to my body. I couldn't wrap my head around the fact that a real live person was growing inside me.

I threw myself into the gift of being pregnant. But a few weeks later, I started to feel off. I can't explain it, but something just didn't feel right. I made another appointment with my gynecologist when I started spotting. The doctor informed me that I was going to miscarry and advised me to return home and allow the process to happen naturally. I was devastated by this news. I withdrew from social interactions and rapidly descended into a state of depression, holding myself accountable for the loss of our baby. I kept questioning myself, pondering if there was anything I could have done differently to prevent this tragic event. The unexpected magnitude of this loss overwhelmed me, inundating my mind with numerous hypothetical scenarios. I couldn't help but feel like a failure, as though my body had betrayed me. Regardless of my efforts to maintain good health and physical fitness, I had not been able to successfully carry a healthy baby to term. The only thing I desired was solitude.

///////

Matt tried to provide comfort and support, but he couldn't fully grasp the emotional and physical turmoil I was enduring. To help me get through the loss, he suggested we move to Pennsylvania. He thought a fresh start might be just what I needed to heal, so we began looking at houses. My mother was also supportive and gave me the strength I needed to persevere. It was a long, hard road, but they both encouraged me that I could get through it. The doctors were also enthusiastic and told me to wait about three months before trying again. I was so excited to be a mother that I desired to start right away. And soon I got my wish when I became pregnant with our son. I was elated to discover the pregnancy, eagerly looking forward to each of my doctors' appointments.

When Christmas rehearsals approached for the new season, I was twenty-one weeks along. After I discussed it with Matt, we thought it best that I take maternity leave from the line. I wanted to focus all my energy on growing my baby and keeping myself healthy and stress-free. I couldn't fathom doing six shows a day with a baby belly. Thankfully, the line was prepared to accommodate my time off.

We had a roster of thirty-six women and the group felt at ease dancing together onstage even as some seasoned dancers retired and new Rockettes joined the team. Each woman was numbered from one to thirty-six, the number representing one's place in order of seniority. The roster guaranteed our positions on the line. Meaning we could take a leave of absence or maternity leave to care for our families, and our jobs and medical benefits were secure. I was thankful to have that security. I wasn't ready to leave my tenure as a Rockette just because I wanted to start a family.

During this time, Matt and I decided to open up a brewery-style restaurant in Pennsylvania. This venture was something Matt had dreamed about and spoke of often. He offered my mother a job as general manager since she, too, had an interest in the culinary business. I was elated that my husband and mother would be working together on a venture they were both invested in. I thought it brought our family closer together. She bought a house in Pennsylvania to be closer to her new job at the restaurant. We were still house hunting but hoped to follow soon.

As my pregnancy progressed, I found myself craving all sorts of sweets, despite not typically enjoying them. I allowed myself to wholeheartedly indulge, loving how my body grew, and seemingly breezed through my final trimester. At delivery, I felt apprehensive. I was not dilating, which resulted in Pitocin—a medication used to induce or strengthen contractions during labor and delivery—being administered. Though I encountered some challenges, two days later than my expected delivery date, my baby boy was born naturally and healthy at exactly 1:00 a.m. in February 1997.

When we arrived home from the hospital, a profound sense of happiness enveloped me as Matt and I entered a new chapter of our lives. Our journey as parents had reached its pinnacle, and the walls of our home now resonated with the completeness that comes with the arrival of a baby. Our families came together to celebrate their grandson.

Eating right and getting my body back into shape reminded me of dance. As I adjusted to motherhood and breastfeeding, I realized how much I missed the stage. I felt like I was in a fog, only sleeping when the baby slept. I started questioning myself as a parent; I often wondered if I was doing the right thing. I didn't know it then, but I was suffering from postpartum depression. Because of this, in spite of missing dance, I just couldn't bring myself to return to the line—or do much of anything, for that matter. The only thing that brought me joy was caring for my son and visiting family.

Thankfully, I had been able to breastfeed, something I had always desired to do. Bonding with him as I nourished his tiny body was a feeling I can't describe. He had a robust appetite, and I felt immense pride in being able to breastfeed after carrying him to full term. However, when he was about two months old, every time he finished feeding, I would burp him, and then he would forcefully vomit everything out. It would end up all over me, him, the chair, wherever we happened to be at the moment. The cleanup could sometimes take up to an hour. This, of course, made running errands and handling day-to-day tasks difficult. Even if I had intended to quickly feed him before heading out to the store, we would invariably be delayed. When I contacted the doctor to express my concerns, they dismissed my worries and told me that I was overreacting. They attributed the situation to the normalcy of babies spitting up. Yet as time passed, our son continued to struggle with keeping anything down and began to appear emaciated.

During his three-month checkup, the concern was evident in

the doctor's eyes. Rather than gaining weight, my son had actually lost weight. They quickly recognized their error in trivializing my previous inquiries. It angers me still that they did not take my concerns seriously and my son had to suffer for it.

They told me to take him directly to the hospital, and I called Matt to meet me there. A surgeon informed us that our son had a condition known as pyloric stenosis, which involves the thickening or swelling of the pylorus—the muscle between the stomach and intestines—and causes severe and forceful vomiting in the first few months of life. It is also referred to as infantile hypertrophic pyloric stenosis. Fortunately, the surgery was a straightforward procedure where the surgeon divided the muscle of the pylorus to open up the gastric outlet. The doctors assured me that he would recover well.

Nevertheless, it was a daunting experience—taking my son into surgery, watching him undergo anesthesia, and the anxious waiting period was a lot to endure. After the operation, the doctor came out into the waiting room and informed us that the surgery had been successful and that our son was recuperating as anticipated. Returning home, I vividly remember sitting in that same rocking chair where I used to feed him, holding him close to my chest, and just crying and crying. I wanted my baby boy to be okay and felt an overwhelming sense of relief that he was now on the road to healing. He was gaining weight, holding things down, and looking so much healthier. The experience was undoubtedly difficult, but the reassurance and bond that followed brought Matt and me closer as parents. Uncertainty and fear gave way to a newfound sense of confidence and unity, strengthening our resolve to provide the best life for our precious child.

Since my mom lived close to the restaurant, I visited with her or spent my days going to the outlets or taking my son to lunch. My dad was traveling quite a bit, his travels leading him overseas. St. Croix was one of the places he frequented, so we spoke here and there but not often. Sometimes Matt would make arrangements for our son so I could have a half day to myself. Still, no matter how hard I tried, I couldn't shake the funk I was in. I was constantly berating myself for being a bad mother. Wondering if I was doing enough to care for him.

A year into my maternity leave from the Rockettes, I found out I was pregnant again. Getting pregnant for a second time filled my heart with such joy and anticipation, as our family was about to grow once more. I had always imagined having a daughter and felt a deep connection with the life blossoming inside me. Every day became a canvas for hope and possibilities as I eagerly awaited the arrival of our little bundle. The bond between us grew stronger with each passing moment, and I knew that regardless of gender, this child would be a cherished addition to our family. As I reflect on this moment in my life, I am filled with immense gratitude for the blessing of motherhood.

Since I was already seven months pregnant when the Rockette season started, I made the decision to take additional maternity leave. My daughter, who was due to arrive in mid-December, came early, clearly excited to start her journey in life. Unlike with my son's birth, she entered the world after just twenty minutes of pushing and was born at 4:40 a.m. in December 1998.

The arrival of our daughter was heaven-sent, but I quickly found myself struggling to manage two small children at home. Matt was preoccupied with the restaurant, so I was with the children most of the time. Starting a restaurant took quite a bit of legwork to get off the ground. There was remodeling to be done inside and outside the building, as well as hiring kitchen staff, back-of-house staff, front-of-house staff, bartenders, and barbacks. Launching a new business demanded a significant amount of focus and dedication, so I understood his need to be away but struggled once more with severe depression. I was a total mess. The stress caused random breakouts and sporadic crying fits. I was repeatedly calling Matt to come home. His absence created a disconnect between us. There was an emptiness inside me that yearned for his presence and the comfort of his embrace. The days seemed chaotic, and I felt as if I was handling everything on my own. Still questioning whether I was being a good mother and with the responsibilities of parenting weighing on me, I wanted his companionship and support that much more. I longed for the intimacy and closeness we had once cherished.

While this was going on, Matt and my mother were having differences on how to run the restaurant. Eventually, after several disagreements, he fired her. This left her with no job, a mortgage to pay, and no family around to support her. Although Matt and I had had plans to move there, we never found the right place to call home. Having no other alternatives, my mother did what anyone would do and filed for unemployment with plans of selling her house and moving back to New Jersey.

As if this wasn't bad enough, Matt contested her unemployment. I had a tough time understanding why he would do this to her. I was so torn between my husband and my mother, I felt like my life was falling apart. Considering separation and divorce is a significant decision even in the best of situations. It had been three long years since I had last danced as a Rockette, and I didn't have a college degree. All I could think about was what would happen next. Could I manage being a single mother of two young children? Moreover, if I stayed in the marriage, how could I justify his actions toward my mother? He should have given her the opportunity to work her way back to New Jersey or, at the very least, given her time to find employment elsewhere before letting her go. I went over it again and again in my head before I made one of the hardest decisions in my life. I asked for a divorce. We were both upset about the situation, but he wasn't coming up with any solutions, and I didn't know what else to do.

Matt appeared to be extremely upset about the separation, though I found out later he had been seeking solace elsewhere. This sealed the deal on our relationship and any notion of reconciling. That Christmas I resumed my position on the line, commuting between New York City and my mother's house in Pennsylvania after daylong rehearsals and shows. My mother and nana helped me with the kids, but the grueling schedule often left me exhausted.

One of my bright moments during this time was when my children first started conversing, becoming real siblings. Their innocent conversations filled my home with such happiness and warmth. Watching them connect and understand each other was a beautiful experience, creating a bond between them that would last a lifetime. As they grew, their conversations evolved, deepening their relationship and leaving a lasting imprint on my heart.

Meanwhile, I was adjusting to my position on the line. The

dancers were much younger and filled with incredible talent. They were working with various choreographers now, not just Violet, whom I had become accustomed to. We were learning a new number that year, making things a tad bit more difficult. It was a lot easier to pick up on the numbers I was familiar with, but the new choreography made it harder to concentrate. I was making so many mistakes, I was pulled aside. They told me that if I didn't get it together, I would be removed from the number altogether. On breaks I'd sit in the corner either crying or calling my attorney. Not only was I readjusting to being back on the line but divorce proceedings added to my mental and financial burden.

I was a disaster.

Eventually, I found a place in Dover, and Matt and I worked out a plan to share seeing the kids on certain days. Though I was glad to have an arrangement in place, it was no easy feat carting them back and forth between New Jersey and Pennsylvania—Matt had finally made the move there—but I was just happy we'd come to some sort of agreement. When the season ended that January, I looked for work for the off-season. I thought bartending might be a good idea, so I attended a bartending school to learn how to make mixed drinks. I found a job at the Chili's in Parsippany and was in for a big surprise. Bartending is much harder than it looks. Making drinks for not just the bar but the entire restaurant is extremely difficult and a lot to remember at once. Plus you're serving patrons at the bar food, drinks, espressos . . . it was really challenging. By the time I got home at 2:00 a.m., my brain was fried, my feet hurt, and I reeked

of booze. I knew I couldn't keep working there, so I began looking for nine-to-five jobs and auditions.

One day, as I was about to walk into a commercial audition, I
received a call from a woman at Child Services. I immediately
thought something had happened. And, yes, something had happened. She told me someone had called their office stating that I
was not a fit mother and should be investigated. My heart stopped.
I tried so hard to be the best mother I could be considering the
situation, even though I sometimes doubted myself. Who would
do this? Could they really take my children away from me? I was
so distracted, my audition ended up being a hot mess. I didn't get
the part.

While working alongside the woman from child services, it became evident that the reported issue was not rooted in genuine
concern but rather stemmed from my divorce. Coming from a
background of handling actual cases of child abuse, she empathized
with me and swiftly determined that this was simply a case that
didn't need further investigation. Because of her duty to investigate
reports of abuse, she dedicated herself to thoroughly looking into
the matter and eventually dismissing it, providing me with assurance and peace of mind.

Altering my perspective, I put my energy back into finding
better employment. By this time, my mother had sold her house
and moved back to Jersey, about five minutes from where I lived.
Since she was close, she was able to help me by watching the kids
when I worked. Soon I was able to secure a gig doing secretarial
work until a more permanent position came through that worked
around my Rockette schedule. I planned to return to the line for

the upcoming holiday season, which would help out tremendously.

On a summer afternoon, as I sat in the backyard, watching my kids playing on a slide I'd gotten at a garage sale, I thought about my desire to perform on Broadway. Flashes of that amazing performance of *The Wiz* and Stephanie Mills ran through my mind. I thought about all the opportunities that would come my way if I got cast for a show. Broadway productions had a better chance of long runs, equating to steady work. Shows like *Cats*, *The Phantom of the Opera*, and *The Lion King* had run for years. I knew of other Rockettes who had left the line to do Broadway and vice versa, so the transition wasn't uncommon. I sat in the warmth of the afternoon sun, meditating on my dream and how I could make it come to fruition, all while being soothed by my children's laughter. They would be so proud of me if I made this happen, and I could be a shining example for them.

I hit the ground running, keeping up with any job boards and resources I could find to stay abreast of castings and auditions. But as I worked toward securing better employment, I began to notice our childcare arrangement weighing heavily on the kids. There were moments when I felt like quitting my job and staying at home with them, but I knew the importance of our family's financial needs. I had to work.

I distinctly recall one Christmas morning when we woke up feeling cold because I had overlooked contacting the oil company. I didn't know anything about refilling the tank and it was a lesson learned. There was just so much happening at once at any given time that it made it hard to remember the simplest of things sometimes. Regardless of the hardships, returning home to my children always filled me with peace of mind. The house felt incredibly empty when they were not around. It was a difficult time, but I held out hope that I'd come to have a civilized co-parenting relationship with my ex-husband for the sake of our kids. I would have loved it if we could have created an environment that allowed us to harmoniously share their important milestones together as a family unit, even if we were no longer together.

///////

In 2001, when the Christmas season concluded, the Rockettes danced at George W. Bush's inauguration. We all took the Amtrak train to Washington, DC, and the highlight of the trip was that I got to meet the new president of the United States and Muhammad Ali, the former heavyweight champion. His giant presence was surprisingly gentle and soft like a feather. The two interactions made a monumental impact on my life and career. On the train ride back, I was struck with thoughts of what I was going to do now that the season was over. With the pending divorce and tons of legal fees, I needed something steady now more than ever.

The revival of the Broadway musical *42nd Street* prompted numerous Rockettes to audition since the season had just ended. I felt apprehensive about my tapping skills and age, so I hesitated to try out, questioning my ability to keep up with the demanding choreography. I had been dancing with the Rockettes for over a decade, so it had been years since I last attended a dance class.

The casting agent put together an audition for minorities, and I received a message on my voicemail upon returning home from DC, asking me to come in. I immediately worried I wouldn't be good enough—I knew there were others who were much better dancers and singers. And then the PR lady from the Rockettes came to mind.

Nobody cares about you. . . . You should consider yourself lucky to even be here.

While I may not have exceptional singing abilities, I am dedicated to honing my strengths, particularly in dancing, and I pushed myself not to dwell on my limitations. That said, a few days later, I participated in an audition where we were taught a brief tap routine before being asked to perform a vocal piece. Since I didn't have sheet music, I chose to sing the "Happy Birthday" song. Despite a few off-key notes, I delivered a commendable performance. As I readied to leave, the casting assistant unexpectedly invited me to wait. A little while later I found myself in a room, being introduced to the show's director, Mark Bramble. He asked about my Actors' Equity card, a union card for stage actors, and I replied that I didn't have one. To my surprise, he promptly offered me a role in the cast and suggested that I obtain the card as soon as possible. I was in disbelief.

Was my childhood dream of performing on Broadway about to come true?

Contrary to when I received the initial invitation to perform at the Rockettes' Super Bowl halftime show, I didn't think twice about accepting the director's offer. Plus it provided the stable income I desired—I earned $1,800 per week. I was now officially a member of a Broadway cast.

///////

My divorce was finalized in 2002, and Matt and I were awarded joint custody of the children. I was thankful that this difficult chapter was now over, especially in light of my amazing new job. But rather than feel a profound sense of relief, I felt devoid of any sensation at all. Perhaps it was because I was mentally preparing for the next shoe to drop.

10

Owning My Power

You know the saying "God never gives you more than you can handle"? Well, I strongly believe in its truth. Though I had felt melancholy about my situation, God had opened the door for me. My prayers, meditation, hopes, and even fears got me the little-girl dream of performing on Broadway and walking out that backstage door just like Stephanie Mills. It also helped that the Rockette roster was still in place, so I was able to take another leave of absence to focus on the production. I was fortunate enough to keep my place on the line and was ready to take a chance and follow my heart toward my Broadway childhood dream.

With a steady income, I had the resources to better provide for my children, which really helped to lift some of the depression I had been feeling. Since I got to work on the production from the ground up, I didn't feel left behind. We were all there to learn and grow as a cast, a team, and I loved the process of it.

While I was basking in the newness of being a Broadway performer, there was a health scare none of us saw coming. My mother received a breast cancer diagnosis. This came as a shock to my family. But instead of allowing it to overtake her life, she remained remarkably composed and continued to support me in looking after my children while undergoing radiation treatment. Even when I was busy with rehearsals, she would either come to my house to care for the kids or take them to hers. She said it helped to keep her mind on more positive things. This provided me with the peace of mind to not only focus on work but know my kids were helping my mom through her diagnosis. Giving her a beacon of hope to grab hold of. Fortunately, with the grace of God, she managed to overcome the illness, though it did leave its mark on her.

//////////

As I dealt with these new changes, I was filled with a deep sense of dread. I was nervous about Matt's reaction to my new job, fearful I'd get another child wellness call. Though I had my mother's support, I wanted to show my children that I was dedicated to being their mother and a part of their lives. Concerns about transportation for the children weighed heavily on my mind, but I figured it out. I couldn't control Matt, but I could control how I handled things.

I was thankful that production was right in the heart of Times Square, making it convenient to get to and from the theater since I was familiar with the area. The people I met and worked with became more than cast and crew but family. We learned from one another. Looked out for one another, had one another's backs. Not only did I learn the ropes from my fellow castmates about what it took to be a great actor and entertainer but I also learned a lot about the production of a Broadway show from the stage crew. We made such strong bonds during the show's run that I am still friends with many of the cast and crew members to this day.

Preparation for the show was everything I had hoped for. I was brimming with excitement to kick things off. The rehearsals resembled those at Radio City Music Hall but with one major distinction—the choreography allowed for more freedom, as we weren't required to dance perfectly in sync. This created an atmosphere for us to showcase our individuality. Rehearsals often extended to eight hours per day, including a dedicated music section where we learned the show's songs and recorded our voices. As singing didn't come naturally to me, I put in extra effort to train and strengthen my voice for the role. The work was incredibly rewarding, marking an extraordinary journey.

Just before the show's start, I stood on Forty-Second Street, preparing to perform for my first time on Broadway. Everything I had worked for was finally coming to fruition. The anticipation of stepping onto the theater stage was invigorating. With each rehearsal, the stage became my sanctuary, a place where I could connect with the audience in ways words alone could never accomplish. This opportunity was not just a career milestone; it was a celebration of resilience and unwavering belief in the power of one's dreams.

On opening night, I invited my mother and nana to join me not only for the show but for the after-party. Their wholehearted acceptance of my invitation truly showcased their support, filling me with immense joy. Given their unwavering assistance, support, and love throughout my divorce, I expected that they would cherish this moment as much as I did. I was right. Having my family present to commemorate the realization of my dreams is a moment that will forever hold a special place in my heart. Their pride in witnessing my dedicated pursuit of a Broadway career was evident, knowing it had been my lifelong aspiration.

The lavish celebration unfolded at the opulent Marriott Marquis in Times Square. The path from the theater's stage door to the venue was decorated with cutouts of the *42nd Street* banner along with confetti and glitter, creating a visually stunning route for the guests. The event took place in a spacious hall adorned with numerous tables and exquisite floral arrangements. The attendees included cast members of the show as well as distinguished figures from the world of Broadway, television, and film. Notably, the esteemed Liza Minnelli was among those in attendance. It felt surreal to be in the same space as her and other icons, all elegantly dressed for the occasion. I wore a stunning, formfitting gown in hues of brown and tan, accentuating my figure as it gracefully swept down to the floor. The ensemble was complemented by elegant strappy heels, and I felt resplendent, perfectly aligned with the ambience of the soirée. It was an evening to remember.

///////

The show brought in folks from various walks of life. I loved stepping through that backstage door and onto the stage to create a whole new world for the audience during our two-and-a-half-hour performance. We had the largest cast on Broadway at that time.

The dressing room held twenty-four ladies, and it was broken down into three "pods" of eight. Getting ready for the show, we'd talk, laugh, and make jokes while I applied my makeup, lipstick and lashes, meticulously. Then I would pin curl my hair into place, add my wig cap, and head to the mic department to get my microphone placed. Once completed, I went to get my opening wig on—I had four wig changes throughout the show—then headed back to the dressing room to put on my costume. I would literally become another person.

One of the dressers was the sweetest. She'd get me dressed, then we'd laugh and joke as I got ready to walk onstage. We were just two women having fun, enjoying the moment and loving our jobs. I got to interact with the audience, which was amazing, whether for autographs or photos. The interactions definitely made me feel nostalgic.

Throughout the summer, Camp Broadway would come to see the shows. It was a camp for kids interested in theater. A few of us would speak to them, reminding me of myself at that age, enamored with the production and its performers.

The news of Julie Andrews in the audience spread like wildfire through the theater. The mere mention of her name evoked whispers of awe and reverence, for she was an icon whose talent and grace had left an indelible mark on our hearts. As the final preparations were made, a palpable energy hung in the air, as we knew that we were about to perform for someone who had illuminated the stage and screen with her unparalleled artistry. The lights dimmed, the overture filled the air, and as the production unfurled before us, I stole glances toward the audience, hoping to catch a glimpse of her ethereal presence. And then, as the curtains descended after the final act, there she was, standing amidst the thunderous applause. Her radiant smile was a testament to the awe-inspiring spectacle she had just witnessed. When I saw her, a surge of gratitude and reverence washed over me, an understanding that she, too, had once stood in this same place, feeling the transformative power of the stage beneath her feet. Julie Andrews coming to see the performance was not simply a surreal moment; it was an homage to the lineage of performers who had graced those hallowed grounds. It reaffirmed the legacy of theater and the unbreakable bond shared by those who understood the profound impact of the spotlight. That evening will forever be etched in my memory as a night when aspiration and reality blurred in the gentle presence of a theatrical icon.

Behind closed doors, however, I was still struggling with bouts of depression and continued to deal with co-parenting issues. The pressure never stopped. The only bright side was that I was able to put a down payment on a house, and my father helped me out with the rest. My dad had always been in real estate, owning and running several properties, so he was quite the expert in that arena. The house was closer to New York, in West Orange, where my aunt and uncle lived, so that made my commute into the city quicker. My mom moved in to help with the kids; this way, she wouldn't have to drive home at all hours of the night, even if it was just five minutes away. With the house, we had enough space for everyone to be comfortable, and my kids could have their own rooms. My mother had separate quarters downstairs, and the kids and I were upstairs. It was perfect. She was a great help, caring for them, cooking, cleaning, and getting them into bed while I worked on the show. We had a great system going. And since my dad had slowed down a bit with his business obligations, he came over often.

Everything was going well until the owner of Madison Square Garden—who also owns Radio City and the Beacon Theater—decided it was time to disband the roster. Doing this would mean there would be no maternity leave, medical insurance, 401(k), or leave of absence for any reason. Every woman would have to audition each year for the show, so that sense of security was now gone. Having that stability had kept me afloat even when everything was falling apart. Yes, I had to get part-time work in between seasons, but I knew I could count on that income every year. I couldn't imagine having to choose between wanting to start a family and keeping my job. Not to mention the lack of medical benefits to support oneself. I always had that to fall back on after the births of my children and even through my divorce. Where would I have been without it?

I joined a group of Rockettes, some former and some current at the time, who formed an initiative to protect the rights of dancers within the Rockette organization. Our purpose was to keep the roster as it was. Many of us spoke publicly to anyone who would listen, including the media and tourists. Several of us were in favor of keeping the roster unchanged, though some wanted to see it changed. There was a clear divide on the issue, but we made sure our voices were heard.

Ultimately, however, despite our best efforts, the roster was broken.

///////

Moving on from the Rockettes was a tough decision filled with conflicting emotions. As much as I loved being a Rockette, I needed stability. I was older now and fully engrossed in my work on Broadway. Balancing the responsibilities of being a parent to two children and having a mortgage to pay was something I was not willing to gamble. As the troupe disbanded, we received a buyout based on our years of dedicated service.

When I received the formal announcement about the roster being dissolved, I found myself sitting in the dressing room, having a big ugly cry. That chapter of my life was now officially closed. The moment was bittersweet.

After resolving our issues with Radio City, I was relieved to go back to my role in *42nd Street*, putting my days as a Rockette behind me. My time at Radio City and the part I played in introducing a new era will always hold a special place in my heart. I am confident that Russell Markert would have taken pride in the Rockettes' evolution and the diverse representation it now embraces.

///////

In addition to adjusting to life on Broadway, I began learning more self-care practices. Oprah had just released her magazine, *O*, and I absolutely fell in love with it. There were several articles at that time about meditation, finding peace, and changing one's perspective for the betterment of their lives. Ultimately, seeking out positivity in your everyday life, trying to have balance, and living stress-free. There were also articles about dating and personal relationships.

One point that stuck out to me was that when someone shows you who they are the first time, believe them. Surround yourself with people who are going to lift you higher, not bring you down. Between Oprah's magazine and uplifting poets like Maya Angelou, I worked hard to change my perspective on how I walked through the world. I was embarking on a new journey, which meant new challenges, but also new ways to find joy.

"Rocking Around the Christmas Tree" opening number
of the *Christmas Spectacular*

11

To Hell and Back

While I was thankful to be working on Broadway, I continued to feel like I wasn't a good mother. I'd receive letters from Matt every time I went to pick up or drop off the kids, and the words on the pages cut through me like a serrated knife. It remained challenging to collaborate on co-parenting while keeping up with my vigorous show schedule. Travel costs and residual legal fees had me consistently working to make ends meet. At the very least, I felt like Matt could meet me halfway and split the driving responsibilities to get the kids back and forth. My heart sank each time I dropped them off, but I loved my children with my entire being and was determined to keep trying, to never give up, and to love them as best I could. One form of therapy that worked for me was writing—journaling, in particular. That, coupled with the magazines I'd been reading, shed a fresh perspective on life. Anytime I felt frustrated, flustered, or ready to give up, I'd find a quiet space and jot down my thoughts. It helped me to be vulnerable and get my stress out on the page without being judged. There

I could be free to let go of the weight of the world that I felt was on my shoulders.

It also helped to have the support of my family. My mother was a shoulder to lean on and someone I could talk to. And since buying the house, my father came over for dinner often or just to hang out. It further proved my point that this was what divorced families could accomplish. . . . Even though I was much older, it felt good to see my parents getting along and coming together to support me.

My father used one of my spare rooms as an office and worked from our house whenever he stayed over. Eventually, he and Mom would announce that after fourteen years of marriage, twenty-three years divorced, they would rekindle their relationship. He ended up moving in with us and bought a piece of property in St. Croix, where he would spend months at a time. He began building a magnificent home in the hills overlooking the Caribbean Sea. My mother would accompany him on some of his travels.

It was nice to see my parents happy. With my family completely settled and in a good place, I was excited to see what the future held for me. Their example showed promise that Matt and I could be civil toward each other one day and be able to celebrate events together for our children.

Living paycheck to paycheck, I never let up on providing a stable home for us. If I had the time and money to spend every waking moment with my children, I would have. As kids, they didn't know or understand that, so our relationship grew strained. Teenage years are hard for every child, especially children of divorce and one as stormy as ours. My son and daughter each handled it as best they could, but the situation took a toll on us all.

Performing on Broadway gave me the peace I needed, and I willingly welcomed the changes in the cast. As some members departed to explore new opportunities, there was a significant turnover and decrease in the number of original cast members I had started with. The new cast brought a youthful energy and fresh perspective, motivating me to adapt and evolve.

As I navigated parenthood, my journey was filled with highs and lows. I was appreciative of my close friends and the time they spent supporting me. They understood the strength it took to hold it together during performances, having witnessed my breakdowns as soon as the curtain came down after the last bows. Once it was so painful, the entire dressing room went silent.

I felt frustrated and utterly drained, but I smiled through the pain. The yearning for my children and the missed milestones in their lives due to my work obligations and custody schedules weighed heavily on me. I began to internalize a multitude of emotions, most of which were negative. I constantly felt like a failure. My sisters were making strides in their own lives and careers, and many of my friends were successful in their professional endeavors, married with children, and seemingly happy with their choices. Even my parents had found their way back to each other. Yet here I was, facing another uphill battle. At least now I had a consistent income as long as the show remained open. And we were thriving. We constantly received glowing reviews for our performance, accuracy, and authenticity. The packed house night after night assured us that we were successfully entertaining the audience. Backstage, numerous patrons expressed their enjoyment of the show, including those who came to see us multiple times.

When a show opens on Broadway, the cast has to be prepared for newspaper reviews as well as reviews for that year's Tony Awards. We all made a conscious effort to bring our A game to every performance. Each time I read a positive review, it boosted me up that much more. It reminded me why I worked hard at my craft; I was meant to be there.

The possibility of being nominated for a Tony Award was exciting. Sixteen individuals or a group from the organization was sent out each year to review the shows. There is a secret ballot system of who will get nominated. There are all sorts of categories, like Best Musical, Best Play, Best Choreography, Best Actress, Best Supporting Actress, and so on.

I couldn't believe a show that I was a part of from the ground up was being considered for this prestigious award. I remember we were preparing for an evening show, and one of the stage managers announced over the PA system that he had big news. We quieted down, hearts pumping with excitement, unsure if what we heard was true. We were nominated for Best Revival of a Musical, and there were a couple actors in our cast who got individual nominations. We were very excited to have these nominations in addition to the overall production being nominated for an award.

To add to our excitement, we found out our show would open for the Tonys!

The fifty-fifth annual Tony Awards were being hosted by Nathan Lane and Matthew Broderick. The preparation was intense and invigorating but nothing like anything I had experienced before. We had rehearsals before shows or in between a matinee and evening show. They were long days, but these moments together were priceless. People don't realize how different working on a live stage is from working on television or film. For the latter, you can do a number of takes until you get it right, or the video editor will just cut that part out or use a different take from the scene. On-stage, however, there are no do-overs. The pressure to get it right is on. If you do mess up, you have to catch the next step quickly and continue on as if nothing happened.

The choreographer wanted the opening for the award show to be engaging and fun, making it appear as if we ran all the way from our Broadway theater at Forty-Second Street to Radio City. We had a taping where we danced from the theater to the train station and tapped our way onto a subway car. Once we arrived at our stop, we got off the train and ran to the hall. The recording would play and hold the audience's attention as we set up throughout the aisles of the theater. This way, once the recording completed, it would look as if we were exiting the train and joining them at their seats. It was a sweet moment for me because I would be performing at Radio City, my favorite theater and dance home for fifteen years. It was kismet.

We opened the show with an infectious energy that sent tingles down my spine. The rush of performing our routine in the aisles, with the audience right there beside us, and then bounding onto the stage to deliver our number was absolutely exhilarating. It was unforgettable. The audience was packed with stars from different Broadway shows—the crème de la crème—and they were loving every minute of it. After our performance, we headed backstage. Since the show was broadcast on TV, we were given cues by the crew for when we could move about the theater. Standing backstage, we were told to wait, as our category would go first. Christine Ebersole won Best Performance by an Actress in a Leading Role in a Musical. Kate Levering and Mary Testa were nominated for Best Performance by an Actress in a Featured Role in a Musical. Mark Bramble, the one who hired me on the spot, was nominated for Best Direction of a Musical. And Randy Skinner was nominated for Best Choreography. When they announced us as the winner for Best Revival of a Musical, we came back out, high-fiving and hugging one another. I remember sitting through the rest of the show in awe of the night, the experience, everything. It is one of my greatest memories.

We attended a Tony Awards after-party. Ours was being held at Bryant Park, and we were the stars of the night. Everyone wanted to meet us, congratulate us, and take our picture. In our gorgeous dresses and heels, suits and tuxedos, we partied and danced the evening away.

It was a magical night indeed.

The Tony win made the show even more popular. As all Broadway shows do, we had a PR firm working with us to get additional media attention, commercials, promo ads, features on some of the actors, and basically anything we could to keep the show and performers relevant. I was one of the chosen few to be featured on the cover of *Playbill* as well as a poster in Times Square. We also did a lot of commercials.

About three and a half years into the run, the cast was called into a meeting at the theater. We met in the house, whispering back and forth about what the meeting could be about, hoping that it wasn't as many of us had feared. When the stage manager began talking, I was even more nervous because his tone was not that of its usual upbeat tenure. Upon hearing the words "the show is closing," I blanked out. Dread filled my heart, and my breath quickened. They gave us three months' notice so we could plan accordingly, but that still didn't feel like enough time.

But as the saying goes, all good things must come to an end. And the end had come for *42nd Street*. The show ran for about four years, from 2001 to 2005, and I was there from opening night to closing night. It was a lot of work to perform each day, traveling in and out of the city, but I cherished every second of it.

I knew I could collect unemployment, but it was a daunting feeling because I could not afford to take care of my family on that money alone. I would no longer have healthcare or any kind of benefits. Auditioning wasn't going to pay the bills, and I had two kids at home plus a mortgage. I struggled with what my life's true purpose really was.

I hit the ground running looking for a nine-to-five job, made more difficult due to my lack of experience outside of dance. My resume was bare-bones, and I didn't have the best office skills. I wasn't sure who was going to hire me. I'd never used a computer for work, so I had no idea how to navigate any of the software programs, and I wasn't the fastest typist. My anxiety was on ten. In spite of my success and having been the first Black Rockette, first Black pageant winner in New Jersey, and part of a Tony Award–winning cast, I was back to square one and asking myself the question my mother had asked me all those years ago. "What are you doing with your life?"

During that three-month period, whenever I wasn't in rehearsal or performing, I was applying for jobs online. I also had to buy office wear. Cute sundresses and workout clothes were not going to cut it. I went to Macy's and got a couple interview suits, a few pants and tops, and a pair of low-heeled shoes. I interviewed at several places, but unfortunately, no one called me back. As the show ended, I was unemployed and frantic about how I would make ends meet.

One of my good friends, a former stagehand for *42nd Street*, notified me of work that was available at his new job for Jazz at Lincoln Center. He was one of few Black men to claim the position of head carpenter. I would set up for shows or sweep the floor, basically doing stagehand work, which was different from performing. I'd often work late nights into the early morning, then do temp work during the day at various companies, performing tasks like typing, filing, expenses, booking lunches and trips, and working front desks. I went with the flow, piecing things together, asking questions, and making the best of each situation. A job was a job, and I appreciated the money, the opportunity, and the ability to add these skills to my resume.

Coping with these changes was hard on me, so I needed an outlet to de-stress. When I started on Broadway, I was introduced to hot yoga, which helped to keep me not only fit but relaxed and mentally healthy. I completely fell in love with the practice and did yoga whenever I could. Whether it was vinyasa or Bikram, I did it all. I'd found a Bikram studio about fifteen minutes from my house, where I would go whenever my schedule allowed. My father was practically living in St. Croix, and my mother was visiting him for months at a time. By then I finally landed a nine-to-five, had weekends and holidays off, and got to spend more time with my children. Interactions with my ex, however, were still difficult and hurtful. It was unimaginable when my children were told to call their stepmother Mom. Or the time I pulled into the driveway to pick up the kids, surprised not to see their cars there. It wasn't until I made a U-turn that I spotted their vehicles parked down the hill, seemingly hidden from view. It was an inexplicable blow that will remain unfathomable to me.

The situation got so complicated that NaNa, a sounding board and wealth of support, would often accompany me to Pennsylvania to pick up and drop off the kids. I never knew what to expect and wanted our interactions to run smoothly. On the drive, we'd have long conversations about her life and my papa. She enjoyed seeing the kids and hearing about their time with their father.

Despite having a New Jersey court order in place, Matt took me back to court to change the custody arrangement as he was now residing in Pennsylvania. He also filed for me to pay him child support. I won both cases, but after paying all my lawyers' fees, I was left with nothing.

I landed a full-time position at a small mortgage company while continuing to work stagehand gigs whenever they came up. This represented the first glimmer of hope for me after a prolonged period of struggle. Initially, my first paychecks helped me catch up on bills, lifting the weight of my financial burdens. However, four months later, in 2008, the subprime mortgage crisis hit, plunging us into a recession. The mortgage company had no choice but to let me go. It was clear my boss was deeply torn up about it, but unfortunately, he had no other option. The company was in dire straits and simply couldn't afford to keep me on board.

This setback brought me right back to where I started.

Without a steady and sufficient income, I felt my hopes begin to dwindle once more. Dealing with the ongoing custody conflict took a toll on my mental and physical health. I was worn down and unsure how to move forward. With all the financial strain I had accumulated, it became increasingly challenging to meet my mortgage payments.

I applied for a position at a jewelry store located in the Short Hills Mall and was hired as the office manager. Having had experience in light administrative tasks at the mortgage company, I believed this role would enhance my resume. My responsibilities included handling incoming calls, managing cash deposits, and logging incoming jewelry and watches. It was an opportunity to work with some of the most exquisite and valuable jewelry I had ever encountered. However, this job turned out to be one of the most challenging due to the lack of professional boundaries set by the store manager. Although I was hired to work in the office, the staff received updated instructions to clean the break room and bathrooms and perform other custodial duties, as the company was reluctant to hire a cleaning service.

While I understood the importance of maintaining a sanitary environment, cleaning toilets was not a part of my job description. I would have been more receptive to it had I been hired specifically for such duties, but that wasn't the case. When I declined, the manager informed me that if I refused to do so, I would not be allowed to use the store bathroom. As a result, I resorted to using the restroom at Nordstrom, located on the other side of the mall, which was a significant inconvenience and total waste of time. Furthermore, the constant fear of having to deal with the rising hostility at work made each day unbearable. It was disheartening to confront yet another individual determined to make my life miserable. Each morning I was filled with a sense of dread and discomfort.

After work, I would take yoga classes to help ease the stress. There I met a sweetheart of a guy named Dillion, who asked me out for a bite to eat one night. As we chatted, we realized how much we both loved the arts. Dillion, a musician, and I connected over our favorite music, theater shows, and artistic interests. It felt like we had found a kindred spirit in each other, and our connection only deepened from there.

Despite the conditions at work, it was still a job, and it helped me to support myself and my family. So I was devastated and somewhat relieved when the store's umbrella company, Finlay Fine Jewelry, went bankrupt, and I was on the hunt for a job again. I just couldn't catch a break. When was my happily-ever-after going to begin? Something had to give. Yes, I had incurred a tough beginning, but my career had been a dream for over a decade. I felt so blessed to have had the opportunities that came my way. Yet now, to be in debt, still fighting with my ex even after our divorce was finalized, and unable to keep a steady job—I never would have imagined I'd be going through this in my forties. This was not what I had pictured for myself. I was supposed to have a stable life, a stable career dancing and doing what I loved, and caring for my children. How had it come to this?

I finally landed a receptionist job at a private golf club two minutes from my house. The club was closed in January, the month I began training, so it was nice to be able to learn the ropes during this quiet time. No kitchen staff, no members, just the bare-bones crew to make sure the club would be in tip-top shape for the re-opening on Valentine's Day. As the assistant I was replacing taught me how to write up parties, a guy dressed in sweatpants, a hoodie, and sneakers walked in. I didn't pay him much attention since I was focused on learning the job.

"This is the chef, Jeffrey," the assistant said, and I looked up at the man. We exchanged pleasantries, and then my focus went back to training. A moment later, Jeffrey looked at me and said, "I know you." I'd heard this line a million times before, so I quickly dismissed it. After we went back and forth for a bit, the assistant mentioned that we lived in the same neighborhood. That was when I recognized him. The cute guy in my area who I would always wave to on my runs. What were the odds? He had a ring on his finger, so he was off-limits. Nevertheless, it was nice to at least know his name. Once he left, I was told that his wife was diagnosed with brain cancer and had sadly passed away a couple years ago, not long after her diagnosis. He still wore his wedding ring. We'd occasion-ally have flirty moments at work, but nothing to overstep my rela-tionship with Dillion. Things had gotten serious, and he had recently proposed.

About nine months into the engagement, Dillion took me to a back booth at Applebee's and said, "I can't do this." I wasn't exactly sure why he broke things off, but I walked away and never looked back. I am always convinced there is a reason for everything. A week later, I was on a date with the handsome chef.

Soon after, the Rock Spring Golf Club was losing members and facing financial challenges. The Montclair Golf Club, a larger private club, acquired Rock Spring. This led to staff consolidation and ultimately resulted in my elimination. Consequently, I found myself once again in search of employment.

I spent the following eighteen months working various jobs, trying to make ends meet. In spite of numerous applications and interviews, I couldn't secure stable employment, leaving me unable to pay my mortgage. Running, attending yoga classes, and spending time with my children were my only sources of comfort during this challenging period.

By the grace of God, I found a job that would pay more than I'd ever made in an office, working as an executive/personal assistant for the CEO of a real estate company. Things were looking up.

///////

I clung to the house for as long as I could, but the mounting bills became overwhelming due to the impact of the subprime mortgage crisis. Unable to catch up on back payments, I was left with no choice but to foreclose on my home. Eventually, I moved into a small one-bedroom apartment in Bloomfield. While it wasn't spacious, having a patio made it a bit more tolerable. Considering its size, the rent was quite high, but more affordable than maintaining a house. I managed to secure a special offer of one month rent-free and fourteen months at the same rate. Meanwhile, my mother had relocated to St. Croix to live with my father while she awaited for a senior community apartment in West Orange to become available.

The pressure was immense, and I began to sense a tightness in my stomach. I attributed it to anxiety and reminded myself to prioritize meditation. Even though I had a well-paying job, every rent payment felt like tossing money into an abyss and watching it vanish. I no longer had an investment to rely on. In the meantime, my boss was making life difficult for me, finding fault in my procurement of supplies, including the specific nuts he required, and my telephone etiquette. I returned to work feeling constantly on edge, hardly interacting with anyone. I felt jittery throughout the day, and each morning I awoke with a sinking feeling in the pit of my stomach. When he eventually fired me, I experienced a familiar mix of relief and distress, leaving my stomach churning. Again and again, I was back to square one.

12

The Calm Before the Storm

s always, my saving grace was exercise. I was still a vegetarian and ran a few times a week, practicing yoga whenever I could. Having been a dancer my whole life, I found the movement felt natural and calmed my nerves. Serotonin levels increase during a workout, which allowed me to think more clearly.

After selling my house, things continued to go downhill from there. My employment status was of major concern, but I tried to remain positive. At least I got to spend more time at home. But the worry that came with financial instability overshadowed the good times. I was glad when my mom finally secured a spot in the senior care apartment building close by; my family was my backbone. We made an effort to get together as often as possible. With my dad in St. Croix permanently, I didn't see him often.

I also had to accept the reality that Matt and I would never have the civil co-parenting relationship I had hoped for. I let go of that notion and moved on. The kids were older now, so my need to communicate with him lessened, and I only interacted with him briefly during pickups and drop-offs. Matt had declined to do any of the driving, leaving me to drive both ways whenever I had the kids. Despite how difficult he made things, I made a conscious effort not to speak negatively about him—our children adored him. The anguish I experienced in those moments . . . I can't even begin to describe. It felt like the world was against me, and it weighed heavily on my mind.

Some time later, I secured a position as an executive personal assistant for a husband and wife in Manhattan, alleviating some of my financial strain. When I started, a colleague pulled me aside to tell me the wife had bipolar disorder, which eventually made working with her very challenging for the entire staff. She would frequently show favoritism, leaving all of us on edge, uncertain of who she would force to be her next confidant. Recognizing the need to reduce my stress levels, I began incorporating more mindful meditation into my daily routine and continued exercising and journaling. These practices became my lifeline, and at times I found myself writing multiple journal entries a day.

I had recently connected with an old friend, Vanessa, whom I first met on Broadway. She had since become a TV writer in California and was well-informed about my journey from being a Rockette to being on Broadway, my failed marriage, and the stress I endured. Vanessa consistently reminded me of my remarkable accomplishments and encouraged me not to be disheartened by the challenges I faced. She suggested that I do something with my journals, mentioning that my life story could be an inspiration to others and even be turned into a film. Initially I was skeptical, questioning why anyone would be interested in my personal struggles;

people encounter problems every day. However, Vanessa emphasized the significance of my unique journey, highlighting that being the first Black Rockette and the first Black winner of the Miss Morris County pageant were significant achievements. She believed that my experiences would resonate with and provide support for others who had undertaken similar paths. It was difficult to recognize my own accomplishments from an outsider's perspective, but my passion for the entertainment industry persisted, and I longed to return to it. I had to take action.

Together, we collaborated on developing a pitch that we could present to producers and television companies. I was thrilled. Working a nine-to-five job made me feel out of my element. This opportunity gave me something to anticipate and be optimistic about. It also allowed me to show my children that I was not a failure.

Months later we got the call that production companies were interested; I couldn't wait to head to LA to meet with Lifetime, BET, and a few others. Unfortunately, that meant I'd have to quit my job, because I had no idea how long I'd be out of town. I was afraid of losing that paycheck. The what-ifs were too grand to ignore. I immediately called Jeffrey and told him the big news. "If I don't go out to LA, I'm just gonna, you know, live with the regret of what could have been. What if something comes out of this?" We spoke a bit more, and he gave me a lot to think about. I knew I wanted to do this; I just hadn't figured out how.

The couple I worked for lived a short distance from their office. I only had a thirty-minute lunch break, but I frequently walked to the nearby park to enjoy my meal in peace and escape the busy atmosphere of the workplace. Spending time outdoors was crucial for my peace of mind, unless the weather didn't permit it. On this particular day, about ten minutes into my break, my phone started ringing. Seeing that the call was from the house, I initially ignored it, assuming it wasn't urgent since they knew I was on break. However, the calls persisted, leaving me to wonder if I had unintentionally made a mistake.

I answered the phone, and the wife was yelling frantically in my ear. Thinking something might have happened to her or her daughter, I ran back to the house. When I got there, she started going off on me about the trees in the backyard of her four-story brownstone. *Her trees?* I thought to myself. I could not believe she had rushed me back from my lunch break because her trees needed to get pruned, and she wanted me to call someone over to take care of it. She explained that she absolutely needed to have sunlight on her back patio and how this task was top priority. Shortly after, she packed her bags and took off to her home in the Hamptons to get away from it all.

A few days later, a tree company came in to work on the trees. They removed as much as they could, but most of the trees belonged to her surrounding neighbors, so they didn't want to cut them without permission. I only nodded and agreed, thinking, *This is what they do, so they know best.*

Upon her return from Long Island, I received a call urging me to meet her at her home. Once again she scolded me like a child. I insisted that the company had assessed the situation and informed me that there was nothing more they could do. However, she was unwilling to accept this. I had to stand there and endure it. Yes, the pay was good, but was it worth all of this? I attempted to confide in her husband, but he treated his wife with kid gloves and disregarded my concerns. While I understood her condition, it did not give her the right to mistreat me or any of the staff members. I gathered my resolve and walked out that day, never to return. This was my opportunity to head to LA, and I was going to take it.

A new worry crossed my mind, however, leaving me feeling anxious. I no longer had health insurance now that I'd resigned from my job. The cost of COBRA medical insurance was astronomical, and I was almost fifty, which meant my policy would cost more. I had noticed my body changing but simply believed it was a natural part of aging. I pushed my concerns to the back of my mind.

I traveled to LA with a show bible featuring my pictures, a bio, and a television show synopsis to use for our meetings. Feeling bloated throughout the five-hour flight, I attributed it to air pressure, nerves, and the like, hoping to feel better upon landing. Having taken out a significant loan for the trip, I rented an Airbnb in Venice Beach for two weeks. I chose to be close to the beach for runs and meditation, staying in a charming house within walking distance of town, where I had easy access to all necessities.

We were set to have our first meeting with a small production company that Vanessa was affiliated with. We had practiced our pitch and were ready to go. Upon introductions and exchanged pleasantries, Steve and Joe were ready to hear our pitch. Once we finished, there was a heaviness in the air and a look of *this isn't going to work* around the room. The wind was knocked out of my sails. Disappointed, we left and got back to work. We visited friends of Vanessa's who were watching her daughter; they were also in the industry. We told them of our visit and subsequent disappointment. We redid our pitch for them, and they gave us pointers—rather, they gave *me* pointers. One of her friends used his personal experience to make his point. He told me a story about his relationship with his father, and as he was speaking, I was engulfed and emotionally taken with what he was telling me. It brought tears to my eyes. The emotional depth that he used to describe his feelings and what had happened was what was lacking in my own pitch. I was missing that connection to the audience. I left there feeling inspired.

We had two days before meeting with Steve and Joe again, and during that time, I ran, meditated, and crafted a pitch that I hoped would create an emotional investment in my story. On the day of our presentation, as we entered the room to introduce our new pitch to Steve and Joe, it seemed as if they had already dismissed us. However, when we presented our revised pitch, they were amazed and completely captivated by our approach. After that meeting, we went to MarVista in an effort to get them interested and on board with our idea.

Their offices were fabulous, and we were escorted into a conference room where there were five directors and content creators waiting to hear us out. Once again, after pleasantries and a few chuckles were exchanged, we started. I went first and spoke about my heart-wrenching story. The room was so quiet, you could hear a pin drop. We had them. Vanessa followed with her television pitch, and they were sold. They wanted to partner with us.

We set up meetings with Lifetime and prepared similar material, only this time we trimmed it down and had my friend speak first. Throughout the pitch, the Lifetime execs asked us questions and seemed genuinely interested. We left there excited and hopeful. Vanessa's management team set up two more appointments, but my Airbnb reservation was up, so I had to find someplace else to stay. I found another Airbnb in Venice Beach and moved my things there. Three weeks had passed, and nothing had been secured. I started missing my family, and my funds were dwindling. Thanksgiving was also right around the corner.

This rental, a garage redone into an apartment, wasn't as nice as the first. It was dark, the TV didn't work, and I didn't feel safe. But I had no choice because I needed to keep my expenses low. Staying there and toiling over the fact that we had these fabulous pitches without anything solid pushed me into a slight depression.

Vanessa came over and, upon seeing the place, got me out of there and into a hotel room in West Hollywood. I finally had a good night's sleep and loved the convenience of the location. I began to feel better after talking to her about my feelings; she was very reassuring. She knew the business well and explained that this process was normal and could take a long time. Nothing was guaranteed.

When we met with BET, the room was filled with about twenty-five people. We pitched the project with the same enthusiasm as we did the previous two, but they passed. I had been in LA for a month, longer than I anticipated, but I couldn't live with the regret of not knowing if this could work. I had to stay and stick it out—pitch as many places as I could before letting this idea go. Once we attended the pitch meetings we had set up, I returned to New Jersey right before the Thanksgiving holiday.

Although Lifetime still hadn't gotten back to us, I remained optimistic. Then I began experiencing intense discomfort, bloating, and constant gassiness, which became my new normal. I suspected a potential adverse reaction to gluten or dairy, prompting me to make changes to my diet. With no health insurance, I relied on drinking tea and getting rest in the hope that the discomfort would subside, but it persisted and even worsened over time. This occurred toward the end of 2017, during a period of temporary employment. Some days I felt like my usual self; others I worried about whether there was an underlying issue. Or was the stress of having only a temp job with no word from Lifetime getting to me?

In January 2018, Lifetime passed on the project. Though it was a setback, I secured a temp-to-perm position as an executive assistant. The role supported three directors on an hourly basis through a temp agency, and I was told I'd be hired full-time in three months. In March I was informed that orientation meetings were at full capacity, delaying my transition to a salary and benefits until mid-April. Feeling undervalued and not receiving the promised compensation, I had no viable alternative but to remain in the position. As soon as I completed the orientation, I would become a permanent employee and receive full benefits, which were far beyond what the temporary offices offered.

Cancer did cross my mind as my symptoms increased, but I quickly dismissed it, thinking I was healthy and exercised, so that couldn't be it. In early March, I went to get a colonic, hoping it was just trapped gas or constipation. I felt such relief after the procedure, I was confident I'd found the answer. I only needed to clean my colon. I made an appointment for another soon after.

However, I started feeling discomfort creep up again. Once my benefits kicked in, I made an appointment to see a gastroenterologist, and she examined me, then sent me over to be scheduled for both a colonoscopy and an endoscopy. Since I had just turned fifty, I had planned on getting a colonoscopy but didn't have insurance. Although I asked to be seen right away, she said the scheduler would have to see what was available. I couldn't understand this given how much I reiterated how uncomfortable I felt. I asked the scheduler to be seen as soon as possible, yet she scheduled me for a few weeks out. "Look at you," she said. "You're healthy. I'm sure it's nothing."

I didn't take no for an answer and proceeded to once again explain my symptoms, stressing the urgency of the situation and emphasizing the need for immediate exams. My urgency was dismissed once more, and the appointment was scheduled for two weeks later. Was it because I was a Black woman that my concerns were so easily dismissed?

Regardless, I had no choice but to wait another two weeks. During that time, all I could think about was how the same situation occurred when my son had pyloric stenosis. I constantly voiced my concerns to the doctor only to have my feelings dismissed. I was frustrated at being constantly brushed off. I knew something was wrong, and waiting two whole weeks for an examination felt like an eternity.

The day finally came, and I was required to have someone drive me to and from the procedure, so Jeffrey said he'd be my designated driver. I was super nervous because I had to be put under general anesthesia. I'd never had a procedure before where I would be unconscious, so that was nerve-wracking to say the least. It only took about half an hour. When the nurse woke me up, I was a bit disoriented, but then the nerves came rushing back. I had this sense of dread in the pit of my stomach that I couldn't shake, no matter how hard I tried. I just wanted the whole thing to be over.

After the allotted time passed for me to orient myself, I got dressed and was given an orange juice while waiting for the doctor, as instructed. I must have been there for another twenty minutes before she finally came into the room. I sat on a school-type desk and chair, awaiting the results. She made no effort to comfort me when she said, "Ms. Jones, you have cancer, and it appears that you have approximately five years left to live. . . . I'm sorry."

My throat constricted and I almost choked on my orange juice. "What?" I couldn't comprehend what she had just told me, let alone the casual manner in which she had delivered it. She repeated herself, and I simply sat there in disbelief. She asked if I wanted her to notify anyone; I said no. I had sensed that something was wrong but hoped that with medication, stress relief, and loving care, I would return to normal. Colon cancer? I could never have envisioned this happening to me. I was someone who diligently exercised, took great care of her health, and faithfully adhered to a vegetarian diet for twenty-five years.

Just like when I had the miscarriage, I was left speechless.

I emerged from the exam room, and Jeffrey was there, as he had promised. I kept the secret to myself and didn't confide in anyone. Much of the reason was my embarrassment and shame at the unexpected turn of events. I had always been seen as the healthy one in my family.

He drove me back to my apartment and dropped me off, and I went inside alone and started to digest the truth of my situation. I was looking forward to an upcoming family trip to visit my father in St. Croix, thrilled that both my children would be joining us for the trip. We had visited the island once before, when the kids were around ten years old. My father had been busy building his house at the time, so we stayed at the Cottages. During our vacation, we had the opportunity to swim in the turquoise waters, indulge in delicious snacks on the sandy beach, explore the charming town center, and even venture out into the lush rainforest, where we discovered a turtle sanctuary. Our days were filled with love, laughter, and plenty of memorable meals together. This time, my sisters and their children would be traveling with us. Knowing that I had only five more years to live, I was determined to make this a trip to remember. I planned to cherish every moment with my family.

In the weeks leading up to the trip, I spent my time in labs, getting scanned, poked, and prodded. I was directed to meet with a local surgeon to discuss next steps. I waited in the exam room until a nurse came in to get a brief history on me. After she left, I took in the doctor's office, decorated with photos of his idyllic family enjoying vacations in various places. When he came in, he didn't give much detail about my colonoscopy results. Instead, he mentioned ordering more scans and told me to expect a call from an oncologist soon. I was shocked. Was that all? He seemed distant and uncommunicative. It gave me a sense that my surgery was more likely a down payment for his next family getaway rather than an effort to save my life.

Jeffrey came over a few nights before my trip. We sat down on the couch and started talking. I made the choice to confide in him about my battle with cancer. I knew I would be sharing the news with my family while away and felt it was important for him to know before I left. I had been undergoing tests in secret for weeks, trying to keep it from everyone. When I finally spoke, the words were barely audible, almost as if I were acknowledging it to myself for the first time. I had to gather my strength and say it again, this time louder, before I broke down in tears in his arms. We stayed there in each other's embrace, sharing our feelings and crying together for the rest of the evening. When he left, I thought about his past heartbreak from unexpectedly losing his wife to brain cancer. I was unsure if this relationship would be too difficult for him to handle, leaving me to face my illness alone.

My children arrived at the apartment the day prior to our departure to the island. I felt immense joy at having both kids with me at last, a sense of completeness warming my heart. There were three fundamental objectives I aimed to achieve during this trip: cherishing quality time with my family, candidly sharing my situation with them, and ensuring that my children understood my unwavering love for them despite the challenges we had faced. My sole aspiration was to have a more meaningful connection with them before departing from this world.

We reached St. Croix and had a wonderful time. I really enjoyed spending time with my family and was committed to repairing anything amiss in my relationship with my children. I needed to take action. No stranger to hard work, I was always willing to roll up my sleeves to get the job done. I would do whatever it took to reconnect with them, especially now that they were teenagers, soon to be adults.

It was nice to see my sisters, their kids, and my parents together. It was a time for family bonding. Yet I was weighed down with my illness during the quiet moments. I wasn't sure if I could handle breaking the news to them, but I knew it was something I would have to do eventually. I felt guilty about burdening everyone during what was supposed to be a joyful time, so I decided not to mention anything until the last day. I knew that once I returned home, I would face whatever treatment the doctor prescribed and a mere five years to ensure my life had meaning and purpose. At night these thoughts engulfed me, and during the day I was resolute in my determination for our family to experience the finest quality time together.

On our final evening on the island, before bed, I informed the kids that I needed to talk to them. It was important to me that they were the first to know. I expressed my deep love for them and how grateful I was that they were both with me on this journey called life. I emphasized that they meant more to me than anything else in the world. Then I revealed that I had been diagnosed with colon cancer and was given a prognosis of five years left to live. I cried intensely, finding solace in the sturdy construction of my father's house, which concealed my wails.

I then went to my younger sister, Peaches. She was lying down with her son after putting him to bed. I softly knocked on her door and asked her to take a walk with me. We sat out on my father's patio that overlooked the Caribbean Sea. Under the cover of moonlight, I told her my diagnosis. Again I cried an ugly cry as she comforted me. I told her I was planning to tell everyone else before leaving the island.

The next morning, I told Cheryl and my parents. The first thing my dad said was "I can't even believe it's you, because you were always the healthy one." And he was right. Even while on the trip, I got up every morning to go running on the beach or go for a swim with my dad while everybody else slept. So it came as a shock. No one had suspected how sick I was. Then my older sister said, "You need to go to Sloan." She was referring to Memorial Sloan Kettering, where my father had been treated for prostate cancer. He'd been diagnosed during my tenure on *42nd Street*, and his surgery took place around the time of the Tony Awards. Although pregnant, Cheryl was there for him and took care of his needs when he had the surgery, so she knew firsthand the great care Memorial Sloan had to offer. I was willing to try anything, since my previous doctor gave me no hope.

On the journey home, I reflected on everything worth living for. I refused to give in to this illness, resolving to do whatever was necessary to prolong my life.

13

The Battle of a Lifetime

As soon as I got home, I found the information for Memorial Sloan Kettering and spoke to someone about seeing a colo-rectal specialist. I had done my research on their website and knew exactly who I wanted to treat me. Immediately, I was met with compassion and grace. The woman on the phone was very nice and more supportive than the previous surgeon's nurse. She told me she would need my medical history—scans, bloodwork, MRIs, etc.—transferred over to them so they could assess my condition and then schedule an appointment. In that call alone, she showed more compassion than anything I'd received elsewhere. The phone intake took half an hour, and she collected tons of information like my family history, a list of symptoms, when I first started experiencing said symptoms, my diet, exercise routine, vitamins, everything. I don't remember ever being asked much of anything at the other office. It was a relief to transfer my medical records out of the care of "Vacation Doctor" and into the capable hands of Sloan.

Once my files were received, I scheduled an in-person visit.

When I walked into the hospital, I could tell they knew what they were doing. It was organized, clean, and the employees showed kindness to everyone—not just the patients but the caregivers as well. Memorial Sloan Kettering is renowned for its expertise in cancer treatment and research. The institution boasts a diverse team of specialized doctors, each focusing on different types of cancers, including throat, stomach, breast, lung, colorectal, and more. At that time, Dr. Iris Wei stood out as the sole female colorectal surgeon, and I specifically sought her care. She collaborated closely with Dr. Elizabeth Won, who became my oncologist. It had never occurred to me that I would utter the words "I have cancer" or refer to someone as "my oncologist," but here we were.

My mother accompanied me to my initial appointment, where we were welcomed by Dr. Wei, Dr. Won, and their predominantly female team. Their presence and manner instantly reassured me of my situation. A nurse told me, "We will do everything in our power to help you through this," and I believed her. She also added, "One day you will look back on this as just a minor blip on the radar. And please refrain from searching anything on Google."

"Too late," I replied with a shy smile. I had already delved into that abyss and was petrified by some of the stories I had come across. However, they urged me to disregard that misinformation and let them take charge of my care. Their compassionate words meant the world to me. They infused me with the encouragement I hadn't even realized I needed to confront and overcome this challenge. Instead of preparing for my death, I began contemplating family gatherings, witnessing my children's weddings, and meeting my grandchildren for the first time; the staff at Sloan offered me the strength and motivation to plan for my life, to truly believe that I would have more years ahead than the mere five I had been given.

Dr. Wei saw me first. She accessed my records, and as any good doctor would, she wanted to take a look-see for herself. The exam room was state-of-the-art. It had monitors, a table that could recline, and a private bathroom/dressing room. She used a small telescope-like instrument to examine my colon. It wasn't as thorough as a colonoscopy, but she was able to see where the tumor was located. Her team of women assisted her during the procedure. She even told me I could look at the monitor to see what was going on in real time. I peeked over at it but quickly became nauseated and told her I would simply take her word for it. We chuckled. She marked the tumor and took pictures of my colon.

After the examination, I changed back into my clothes and went with my mom to Dr. Wei's office. We sat across from her before she settled back and inquired, "What did your previous surgeon tell you?"

I responded that he had not provided any information. Her astonishment was evident as she exchanged a quick glance with the nurse practitioner and shook her head. Retrieving a pen and paper, she proceeded to sketch a diagram. "Here is your colon, and your tumor is located at the upper part of the sigmoid colon." She outlined the diagram from top to bottom, enlightening me on the sigmoid colon—the terminal segment of the colon, linking to the descending colon and rectum. Its function is to retain stool until it is ready for elimination. With this detailed illustration, I now had a clear understanding of the location of my cancer. Subsequently, she said, "You have stage-three colorectal cancer. Therefore, an immediate start of chemotherapy treatment is imperative."

Tears welled up in my eyes, a mix of fear and relief washing over me. This was the first glimmer of hope I had experienced in months. She mentioned the possibility of needing a colostomy bag in the worst-case scenario, but I expressed my reluctance about it. She assured me that she believed the tumor was positioned high enough that a colostomy bag might not be necessary, though it was too early to guarantee anything. Until that point, I had been independent and active. While recognizing its lifesaving potential, I thought having it might make me feel as though I couldn't savor the few remaining pleasures in life. She told me she would do her best to respect my wishes.

Mom and I then went to sit with Dr. Won, and she explained how we were going to try to shrink this massive tumor. "We're going to start you on a treatment plan called CAPOX, which is a series of chemotherapy treatments. It's oxaliplatin, an infusion, and capecitabine in pill form. You'll do four rounds, and then you'll come back to see me and Dr. Wei, and we'll see how your body is taking to the treatment." I was scheduled to begin chemotherapy.

Some patients preferred to do treatments at home, meaning a port would be inserted into your chest and you'd receive the oxaliplatin treatment directly into your bloodstream for an entire weekend. This could be done safely at home, but I chose to do my infusions intravenously in the hospital.

The start of every treatment began with an infusion for two and a half to three hours. Then I would do fourteen days of pills: two pills in the morning with food, and two pills in the evening with food. After two weeks, I would wait a week, then start the process over again.

Now that my temporary position had become permanent, I had to inform my boss and HR about my situation, which I did two days after my orientation. I didn't disclose the specific type of cancer I had, but I did request accommodations for my treatment. The only colleague I confided in was another executive assistant, Shelly. We had developed a strong friendship, and I trusted that she would keep my condition confidential. I valued my privacy and greatly preferred to keep personal matters to myself. Additionally, I was apprehensive about potential changes in how others might treat me, as well as the unknown effects of the treatment.

My boss was very accommodating and never made me feel any kind of way about needing time off to take care of myself. He told me to do whatever I needed to do. The plan was to work a half day before my infusion, then the following day I would take a personal day. I would spend the day at the hospital, then return to work the next day; it was a schedule that would help me work through the process.

When I went in for my initial round of treatment, I felt incredibly anxious. I had researched this phase of the procedure online and read about the various side effects of chemotherapy, such as hair loss, weight loss, pain, and loss of appetite. This left me unsure of what to expect. However, I reminded myself that my doctors had advised me to entrust them, not the internet, with my care.

My mother accompanied me, and I was grateful to have her by my side. I underwent check-in procedures and bloodwork, and I weighed in at 115 pounds. I had not realized that adjusting my diet to address the dairy and gluten issues I thought I'd had resulted in such a significant weight loss. Due to my small veins, there was always some difficulty in locating the right one for lab work and infusions. The Sloan nurses are some of the best in the country, taking care to use different methods to take blood and make sure the same injector could be utilized for the infusion. Sometimes they would put a warm pack on my arm or hand to help the blood flow better. And if my veins were too small, they would use a pediatric needle. The most important thing for them was to take good care of me. Following the blood tests, I was ushered into a private room, where I settled into a recliner-like chair and was given a warm blanket before the IV was inserted.

Around an hour into the intravenous treatment, the nurse remarked, "How are you feeling? There's a war going on in there now." I glanced at my stomach in disbelief, as I did not sense any of the effects of this ongoing battle. I had been anticipating nausea or immediate frailty, but none of that manifested.

Time went by quickly, and by the end of it, I was surprised by how great I felt. I was actually starving and couldn't wait to get something to eat. Honestly, it was the best I'd felt in months. I was excited to be hungry for food. It was a familiar feeling . . . a forgotten friend.

When I left, I was not only feeling good but I also looked good, because I was confident that I was on the right path. I made sure to have my nails and hair done, and was determined not to let cancer defeat me. This was a routine I followed every time I went in for chemo. I called it my "date day" and made sure to dress to impress when I went in for treatment.

Upon leaving the hospital, we went to an Italian deli in Montclair. I got an eggplant rollatini, pasta, and some bread, even though I had diagnosed myself with a gluten allergy. Oh my God, I went home and ate everything. It was so good; I had lost touch with the joy of savoring food, and my stomach didn't churn the way it used to upon eating. Finishing my meal, I sat back and was like, *Okay, now I have to wait until I feel sick or throw up*. I just knew my stomach would go crazy again. But it never did. I continued to feel fine throughout the rest of the evening.

The next day, I got up and went to work. A nurse from Sloan called to check in on me and asked how I was feeling. It was unreal how good and energetic I felt. I proceeded with the two weeks of pills religiously.

With each hospital infusion, however, I became increasingly fatigued. I would either book an Airbnb near the hospital or wake up early to go for my oxi infusion. Since I had decided against getting a port, I had to constantly switch arms because my arm became stiff and rigid, almost like a brick. I had to massage it to restore blood flow. It was painful and uncomfortable. Other symptoms included the constriction of my throat, loss of pinky toenails, discoloration and slipperiness on the bottoms of my feet, and extreme sensitivity to cold. My treatments began in June, but even a gentle summer breeze would irritate my skin. I had to remain covered at all times and keep a pair of cotton gloves near the refrigerator. I couldn't touch anything cold and avoided cold food and drinks. Fortunately, I didn't completely lose my hair, but I did experience some thinning and shedding.

After four rounds of chemo, I went back to see the surgeon, and she examined me with the same look-see telescope. She encouraged me once more to look at the monitor, but I just couldn't stand the sight of my insides. Once the exam was over, I got dressed, then sat with my mother for the news. Both Dr. Wei and Dr. Won came in to give me an update. Dr. Wei was the first to speak: "Jennifer, what are you doing?"

I was confused. "What do you mean?"

She said, "Your results are amazing. The tissue looks almost completely healthy. You can't even tell where the tumor was. The only way I'm able to tell is because we marked it." I couldn't believe my ears, but she had this big smile on her face and was waiting for an answer. I had to snap out of my reverie so I could give her the response she was waiting on.

"I've been maintaining a healthy diet, and I'm still meditating, envisioning a healthy white or emerald light correcting my cells. I'm keeping up with yoga, taking wheatgrass shots daily, and drinking fresh vegetable juices. In addition to that, I've reevaluated my entire life and removed stress wherever I could. Realizing some relationships no longer served my well-being, I decided to cut ties."

"Well, whatever you're doing, keep going, because it's working." She showed me side-by-side pictures of the angry brown colon I had when I first arrived and pictures just taken of the white and nearly healthy tissue. The news was incredibly positive, and I was happy to be making progress. I was filled with excitement and started to believe that perhaps surgery wouldn't be necessary.

In the process of dealing with cancer and planning treatments, the expert doctors at Sloan held discussions to review their cases weekly. They collaborated to determine the most suitable treatment plan for each patient moving forward. I was informed that the board would convene the following week, and Dr. Wei would update me on our next course of action.

I waited two days before I got a call, but it wasn't from Dr. Wei; it was Dr. Won. She told me they wanted me to do another four rounds of chemo, which broke my heart. I just cried and cried because I was so tired. With each treatment I felt worse and wasn't sure how I would last another four rounds, especially with the oxi. The doctor told me they wanted to make sure the cancer was dead beyond recognition. I pulled myself together, chose to move forward, and put on my battle gear.

My apartment lease was up for renewal with an increase in rent, and with the unexpected and unbudgeted medical bills that were accumulating, worry set in again. I talked with Jeffrey, and since we had been dating steadily, he opened his arms and his home to me. I moved in with him in August 2018.

Understanding my discomfort, Dr. Won encouraged me to do at least two more rounds of infusions at a slower drip time of three to four hours, then continue the last two rounds of pills on their own. That sounded doable to me. In November I ended my chemotherapy and was told I'd need to schedule surgery soon. So much for my thoughts of not having to have surgery. Dr. Wei gave me options of before or after the holidays. I wanted to get it over with, so my surgery was scheduled for December 18, 2018. Before my surgery, I underwent measurements for an ileostomy and colostomy bag, which involved the placement of adhesive circles where a port would typically be inserted. It was a surreal experience to walk around with these circles on my stomach for days, a tangible reminder of the impending procedure. Days passed by filled with prayers and tears as I fervently hoped that Dr. Wei would be able to piece me back together.

I let my job know that I was going to need short-term disability, and we quickly got a temp to cover me. There was just enough time for me to train her before taking my leave.

When the day came for surgery, Jeffrey drove me to Manhattan. I was taken into a room to get prepped—gown on, IVs in place, hair braided so it would stay out of my way during recovery. A few members of the team of doctors, surgeons, and nurses came in and introduced themselves beforehand; they would be assisting Dr. Wei. I gave them a quick reminder that Dr. Wei and I had discussed that I would not be getting a colostomy bag—she would be using extra staples to connect my intestines together. Each of them smiled, as we all knew we would have to wait until she got in there for this to be determined. They humored me anyway.

Once the time had come, they wheeled me into the operating room, which was, again, surrounded by monitors. They pointed to a chair and a huge contraption on the other side of the room. Dr. Wei would be there performing the partial colectomy/bowel resection via laparoscopic surgery. The procedure would take five to six hours. She explained she was going to check my organs, take out nodes surrounding the tumor to make sure we got everything, then check my sex organs to ensure the surgery wouldn't affect anything. She stressed that, as women, we have a number of different cancers that can affect our sex lives and sexualities. Sometimes surgery to the bowel or back passage (rectum) can cause nerve damage. She wanted me to be aware of all the risks and to assure me she would be thorough.

After I was settled on the operating table, they had me count backward from ten, then the next thing I knew, I was being woken up. "Jennifer, wake up. Surgery is over!" I groggily turned my head and could barely keep my eyes open. I was surrounded by the entire team standing at the foot of my bed, smiles on their faces. I couldn't speak but lifted my right hand and patted my stomach. I remember a tall, blond, blue-eyed male doctor who spoke loud and clear: "NO BAG." Relieved, I let my head flop to the side, and I slept for another four hours.

After recovery, Jeffrey accompanied me to my hospital room. Dr. Wei assured me that I could eat whatever I wanted, despite my concerns about dislodging a titanium staple. She guaranteed it was safe to resume normal eating and that I should anticipate passing gas soon, emphasizing that this was a normal part of the recovery process. The blond doctor entered the room next. I was still feeling drowsy when he asked me a series of questions, mostly related to my well-being and pain levels. There was a moment when he made a humorous comment, and although I can't recall his exact words, I remember laughing and being immediately struck by pain. My giggles were restrained while he apologized, but I was still in good humor. Laughter heightened the pain from the seven incisions I had undergone, and I tried hard to contain myself, but his jovial demeanor was catching.

I shared a room with an older woman who was there for longer than I was. There was a male nurse who looked Native American, Roberto. He had long, silky black hair, which he wore pulled into a low ponytail, and he was washing her, giving her water, and brushing her hair. After getting her settled, he came over to me and asked, "Do you want to get up? Walk around for a bit?" Although I was tired of lying down, I quickly said no. I was terrified. I knew I was being held together by staples and was too scared to move; I didn't want anything coming between myself and a full recovery. He said okay and left me there. A couple hours later, I rang the bell, ready for Roberto to return and ask if he could help me walk. The nurses encouraged you to get up and move around immediately after surgery. No more lying in bed for weeks like in the olden days. He arrived with a small pink bowl and washcloth. He was so patient with me and told me not to use my abs but to lean on him. He put his shoulder down, and I placed my head in the crook of his neck as he raised me to a sitting position. I sat there getting my bearings while he took the cloth and dipped it in the bowl of warm water and washed my face. It felt so good. He dipped it in again, and I leaned into his gentle wipes.

One of the routines on the colon recovery floor is walking laps, so I'd see people walk by my room all the time. Some slow, some speed-walkers. Feeling refreshed, I took my IV with me, and Roberto and I began walking together. We traveled down the hall, starting on our first loop. Though I was moving at a snail's pace, he encouraged me to keep moving forward. He was very comforting. I would walk several times a day, and sometimes my mother would join me as well. There was one patient speed-walking around me with his IV walker so fast, I wondered if I would ever be able to walk that fast again.

After two days in the hospital, I was finally discharged and sent home. During my recovery, Jeffrey provided invaluable assistance, as it was expected to be a lengthy process. I didn't want to worry my kids while they were in college, so I kept my cancer journey private. I wanted to make sure they could focus on their studies and enjoy their time without feeling burdened by my health issues. It was important to me that they felt free and independent, so I stayed strong for them and drew strength from my love for them.

Christmas and New Year's were joyously celebrated with a deep sense of gratitude. Then, in January 2019, Dr. Wei phoned me with a final update on the surgery. She delivered the incredible news that I was officially free from cancer. I couldn't contain my joy. In just a short span of time, I went from having a mere five years to live to completely defeating the disease. There was simply no greater feeling than this.

Hearing the news, Jeffrey and I felt optimistic and started envisioning our future together. Although we had a challenging journey ahead, having him by my side had truly been a blessing. His affection and encouragement helped me navigate numerous difficult moments.

We got engaged and were ecstatic about being together.

Meanwhile, I focused on my recovery. I was still a bit sore and not moving at my regular pace. I continued to eat healthy but put an emphasis on getting my weight up. I could barely do a lap around my kitchen, dining room, and living room, much less in the neighborhood. The smallest amount of movement would have me lying down for an hour because I was exhausted. I thought, *How did I ever run for forty-five minutes straight?* But I had to give myself grace. Take baby steps, little by little, and work in small increments. A few minutes here, a few minutes there, until I worked up to walking around outside.

During Jeffrey's free time, we would visit IKEA or the mall, strolling around, providing me with the physical activity I required. Due to the winter weather, I spent my time predominantly indoors or at the mall, as I was cautious about the potential risk of slipping on ice or snow. As winter drew to a close, I managed to venture approximately a quarter mile away from my house and was immensely satisfied with my success. Following the conclusion of my six-week short-term disability period, the time had come for me to resume my duties at work.

Some team members were happy to see me. They couldn't tell that there was any difference in me. Others were not happy about my time off. I collaborated with approximately five executive assistants, and together, we ensured coverage for one another, particularly during absences. I'd even attained the required temporary coverage upon the start of my disability. On the day of my return, I was summoned to HR due to exceeding the permitted PTO days while taking half days and full days off for chemotherapy. The HR representative advised me to discuss my cancer diagnosis with my co-workers in hopes of easing the tension in the department. However, I found this suggestion unjust. My health status was a personal matter, and since my time off had been approved, that information should suffice for my colleagues.

In closing, HR notified me that I was now subject to a stricter set of rules compared to my co-workers. I expressed that this was unfair and emphasized the importance of these rules being universally applied. However, the woman simply shook her head and re-iterated that it was the status quo.

I decided to reach out to an attorney to understand my rights

team anticipated. The circumstances could have been far more challenging, and I am aware of this every single day. Without the unwavering support of my family and friends and the prayers from my uncle Bobby and his prayer group urging me to keep fighting when I felt like all hope was lost, I cannot imagine where I would be today. For them, I will be forever grateful.

14

Becoming Spectacular

There is a common belief that being a pioneer in a certain endeavor automatically brings great rewards or advantages. Life is a dazzling spectacle filled with starlight, sunshine, mythical unicorns, and colorful rainbows. You glide through a swirling mist of smoke and dry ice, your theme song booming in the background as the crowd goes wild. However, I must inform you that it is none of the aforementioned options.

Smashing through barriers and paving the way for others requires a special blend of bravery and perseverance. Being a pioneer involves breaking down stubborn barriers, challenging closed-minded people, and navigating instances of racism and prejudice. This journey often includes facing ongoing resistance from individuals who are unwilling to embrace change.

It's believing in your dream—that you can be and do whatever it is that you love.

Growing up, I learned about diversity and inclusion and the importance of considering others, not just yourself. We are stronger when we embrace other cultures and people from all walks of life. I was often made to feel like it might be safer to dream small . . . keep my light dimmed, not reach for my full potential of performing on a big, bright stage.

The marriage I believed was perfect turned out to be a valuable lesson in setting boundaries. Filled with its own set of challenges, that union gifted me two amazing children.

When facing cancer, I dealt with doctors who overlooked my symptoms and failed to devise a treatment plan, as they had already lost hope for me. It was suggested that I should have surrendered and accepted my situation, particularly considering the higher susceptibility and mortality rates among African Americans with colon cancer.

Facing the disease compelled me to shift my perspective and deeply evaluate my life. It became clear who stood by me and who did not. What I also discovered was that I had neglected myself. Inspired by Maya Angelou's words "If you don't like something, change it. If you can't change it, change your attitude," I took decisive action. I dedicated myself to recovery and began a journey of self-discovery. I am so glad my village did not accept that dismal outcome, and encouraged me to seek other resources.

To everyone who has walked one step, a thousand, or has been on the continuous journey with me: thank you. You've seen me fall, crumble, and rebuild. Like flowers, something will grow from all you've gone through, and what is left is an amazing and beautiful you.

I am grateful to those who doubted me, said I couldn't make it, and made my life challenging. Your influence is sincerely appreciated. Without you, I wouldn't have built the strength and determination to pursue my dreams despite the imperfections in my life. While I've encountered racism and microaggressions, I've realized that everyone carries their own burdens. Dwelling on these burdens keeps one trapped in the past instead of moving forward. Forgiving those who hurt me, as well as forgiving myself for past mistakes, has been a lengthy process. However, it has allowed me to see the positive aspects of life and remain true to myself. I've learned to have faith in my abilities and seize every opportunity, even when the road is challenging. It has been a journey filled with hardships, but I am grateful for the lessons learned.

As I age, I feel more alive than ever. While some regrets linger, I have chosen to accept and learn from them, understanding that we all make mistakes. My primary focus now is to nurture my mental and physical well-being; foster strong and loving relationships with my children; cherish my friends and family; shower love upon my steadfast husband, who has supported me through the toughest of times; and continue to grow. Embracing life to the fullest without any inhibitions is the best way to honor the time we have on this planet.

My sincere hope is that, after reading this book, you will reflect on your own life, acknowledge your potential, and recognize the significant contributions you can make to the world. It's crucial to let go of your burdens and use them to inspire and drive you forward rather than hold you back. Prioritize your mental and physical well-being, whether through exercise, therapy, or meditation—whatever brings you peace and a healthy mind. Shift your mindset and value everything you have, as well as the love and support from those around you.

Becoming spectacular means embodying the finest version of yourself. There were numerous occasions when I felt utterly depleted, not just physically but mentally and emotionally as well. I recall waking up in tears, crying uncontrollably in bed. I felt completely drained and believed that I had no energy left to fight. However, one strategy that has helped me endure is allowing myself one day to assign blame. I express my frustrations, attributing fault to everyone and everything for my circumstances, and then release my tears. I grant myself the freedom to experience my emotions, because I realized long ago that suppressing feelings can corrode you from within and eventually engulf you. These emotions require acknowledgment and validation. Then, the following day, I compel myself to regroup, rally, and identify the necessary actions to resolve the issues I may be confronting.

I harbored numerous unidentified and unacknowledged thoughts and beliefs about myself for an extended period of time, carrying a great deal of fear and insecurity in my stomach over the years. The extent to which our mental states affect our physical well-being is, I believe, often underestimated. It is imperative to cultivate mental fortitude in order to navigate challenging periods. Moreover, each individual must discover a coping mechanism that suits them, as everyone processes trauma differently. Irrespective of the approach chosen, it is crucial to expel negative energy and transform it into something constructive and beneficial. Bear in mind that we cannot always tackle challenges alone. Do not hesitate to seek support from friends, family, a community or spiritual leader, or a therapist. Having the right support system can significantly aid the healing process.

Celebrate all successes, regardless of size. As you start ticking things off your mental (or physical) list, you'll begin to feel better and move in the right direction. It's okay to be angry, but we can't stay angry forever. We need to work through anger, sadness, and hurt to reach the other side. Although it may sometimes seem as if everyone around you is successful and without issues, trust me, they have their burdens, too. No one, not even the wealthiest person on the planet, can escape burdens, strife, and struggles. We all have a different story, a different message, and a unique impact on the world.

I had long been informed that my desires were not attainable. Reclaiming my strength, I embarked on a journey to determine my contribution and how I could make a positive impact. As I persevered, my life overflowed with abundance. This process continues to be a learning experience for me, even with this book. A single sentence or phrase has the power to profoundly impact someone, providing the motivation needed to move forward. During challenging times, recalling a simple phrase may offer solace, just as it did for me. The songs, biblical verses, and uplifting words I received during moments of adversity began to drown out the negativity I had faced.

I am content knowing that my children have grown into accomplished adults with abundant opportunities to pursue their aspirations. My mother, who has consistently been my pillar of support, still resides in a senior community nearby, and we stay in regular contact. My sisters and their children are thriving, and we gather whenever feasible. We uphold a resilient family connection and support one another, even when separated. Additionally, we frequently visit my father in St. Croix.

Once more I am filled with excitement for my work and am thoroughly enjoying cherishing my husband. The profound awareness that my experience as a Rockette has paved the way for more women of color to pursue their dreams brings me great joy. Witnessing the Rockette line evolve to embrace beautiful women from a diverse mix of backgrounds, including young mothers, is truly inspiring. It marks a significant shift in our collective consciousness and history. While there is still room for improvement, I take immense pride in the distance we have traveled. I wish for people to comprehend that it's absolutely acceptable to stay true to oneself and not conform to others' expectations. In the realm of personal growth, we must acknowledge that being in a state of discomfort often serves as the catalyst for transformation. It is in those moments of unease and uncertainty that we truly find ourselves and our potential. The journey of self-improvement encourages us to embrace our imperfections and recognize that they are not flaws but rather intricate parts of our unique selves. In this ever-evolving pursuit, we come to appreciate that it is okay to feel unsettled at times, for it is within this discomfort that we often grow and flourish. It has empowered me to find my voice and establish healthy boundaries. There is so much more I aspire to accomplish, but I am celebrating the progress I have achieved thus far.

Becoming spectacular involves allowing your inner radiance to shine brightly. Pay attention to your instincts and develop your distinctive contribution to society. Recognize that you have value just as you are. To boldly, magnificently, astonishingly, and miraculously move forward.

Life is full of challenges and valuable lessons, and growth often comes from overcoming these obstacles. Just like diamonds, which are extracted from rough conditions, processed, polished, and refined before they reveal their true beauty, everything in life requires effort and refinement. Personally, I aspire to create a legacy that brings me pride and that my family can also take pride in. Furthermore, I hope you feel inspired and find the motivation to help others on their journey, recognizing that each of us is unique and valuable, like a precious, exceptional gem waiting to shine on the world's stage.

ACKNOWLEDGMENTS

With heartfelt gratitude and eternal love:

To my dear mother, Linda, your steadfast support, belief in my dreams, and encouragement have shaped me into who I am today. Thank you for fostering my love for dance and leading me toward the stage, where my soul radiates. To my father, Booker, I appreciate all your tireless efforts to provide for us, ensure we have shelter, and enable my dance journey. My love and gratitude for both of you surpass any words I could express.

To my son, Zachary, and daughter, Isabella—it brings me immense pride and joy to see the remarkable individuals you have blossomed into. I am truly grateful for the beautiful young adults you have become, and my love for both of you knows no bounds.

To Cheryl and Peaches, my sisters in strength and resilience—walking alongside you through life's joys and struggles has been a priceless gift. Together, we stand as the formidable Jones sisters, bound by an unbreakable bond of love and solidarity.

To my ancestors and beloved grandparents—your legacy of fortitude and wisdom is the cornerstone upon which I stand tall. I honor your strength, endurance, and guidance. I know that your spirits guide me through life's triumphs and trials.

To Broadway Dance Center and the late Frank Hatchett—my sanctuary of growth and self-discovery. Within your walls, I found solace, courage, and a canvas to paint my dreams upon. Your mentorship and inspiration have sculpted my path with grace and precision.

To Jeffrey, my cherished partner—your unwavering support, faith in me, and calming presence have been my constant anchor and guiding light. In your arms, I find comfort, joy, and an endless love that fuels my ambitions and brightens my path.

To Johanna, my literary agent, thank you so much for all your hard work and dedication in finding a home for my story. Your belief in its importance has meant the world to me. I appreciate your support more than words can express. Thank you for guiding me through this storytelling journey.

To Patrik and Francesca—your vision and faith in my narrative have given life to the words that convey my journey. To the entire HarperCollins team—your passion, diligence, and unwavering commitment have breathed existence into my story on the pages. Each of you has played an integral role in this beautiful journey.

To Latoya: I appreciate your ability to capture my emotions in words. Your enthusiasm, empathy, and artistic talent have turned my personal story into a touching melody that connects with others.

To the iconic Madison Square Garden and the legendary Radio City Rockettes, I am immensely grateful for the life of love, the challenges, and the doors you have opened for me as the first African American Rockette. Every moment I spent walking through the golden backstage doors and rehearsing in the large rehearsal hall steeped in history since 1932 is etched in my heart. Dancing on the famed Radio City Music Hall stage was a dream come true, and I feel blessed to have paved the way for other Black women to proudly call themselves Radio City Rockettes.

To every soul who has touched my life, whether in a fleeting moment or a lasting bond, your presence has woven a tapestry of support and love that envelops me in gratitude. Each step of this transformative journey has been illuminated by your kindness, guidance, and belief in the power of storytelling. Your contributions, no matter how seemingly small, have shaped this dream into a beautiful reality that I hold dear. With heartfelt appreciation and a heart brimming with thankfulness, I acknowledge each one of you for being an indispensable part of this extraordinary chapter in my life.

Thank you all for this incredible opportunity to create change, break barriers, celebrate diversity, and make history. Your support and love have empowered me to stand proudly as a beacon of inclusion and excellence.

With deepest appreciation and boundless love,
Jennifer Jones

ABOUT THE AUTHOR

Jennifer Jones is a trailblazing dancer whose inspiring journey unfolds beautifully in her memoir, *Becoming Spectacular*. As the first African American Radio City Rockette, she broke barriers and made an indelible mark on the stage. Her exceptional talent also graced the cast of the acclaimed Broadway production *42nd Street*, which garnered the prestigious Tony Award for Best Revival of a Musical.

Beyond her achievements in the spotlight, Jennifer is a passionate advocate for equality in the arts, championing inclusivity and representation. A courageous warrior, she conquered colorectal cancer and uses her experience to raise awareness about early detection and screening. She is a beacon of hope and resilience.

Jennifer's creativity shines through her writing, exemplified in the heartfelt children's book *On the Line: My Story of Becoming the First African American Rockette*. Her artistic vision flourishes in the enchanting Dancing Jenn Doll, a physical representation of her unwavering dedication and heartfelt desire to inspire others to believe in their dreams.

Jennifer resides in New Jersey with her husband, Jeffrey. Her life radiates resilience, creativity, and unwavering commitment to advocacy and artistry. *Becoming Spectacular* invites readers on a transformative journey, showcasing the power of perseverance and passion in shaping a legacy that transcends the spotlight and resonates with empowerment, authenticity, and the pursuit of spectacular dreams.